# Math in Motion

## FIRST STEPS IN MUSIC THEORY

ANSWER KEY
SECOND EDITION

Caleb Skogen

WITH KYLE BAILEY

Caleb Skogen with Kyle Bailey, *Math in Motion: First Steps in Music Theory, Answer Key,* second edition

First edition published 2015. © 2017 Classical Conversations® MultiMedia, Inc. All rights reserved.

Published by Classical Conversations® MultiMedia, Inc.
255 Air Tool Drive
Southern Pines, NC 28387
www.ClassicalConversations.com | www.ClassicalConversationsBooks.com

Cover design by Classical Conversations. Cover image: *Music and Literature,* William Michael Harnett, 1878. Courtesy of the Albright-Knox Art Gallery, public domain.

All Scripture quotations, unless otherwise noted, are taken from the King James Version of the Bible.

Printed in the United States of America

ISBN: 978-0-9984373-7-8

 # Table of Contents

EXERCISE and REVIEW ANSWERS

    CHAPTER 1—Fundamentals of Music: Pitch ........................................................5

    CHAPTER 2—Introduction to Rhythm ..............................................................17

    CHAPTER 3—Simple Meter ................................................................................24

    CHAPTER 4—Compound Meter .........................................................................33

    CHAPTER 5—Scales .............................................................................................41

    CHAPTER 6—Key Signatures ..............................................................................51

    CHAPTER 7—Scale Degrees and Transposition ................................................59

    CHAPTER 8—Intervals .........................................................................................69

    CHAPTER 9—Triads and Triad Qualities ..........................................................79

    CHAPTER 10—Triads: Roman Numeral Analysis .............................................85

    CHAPTER 11—Triad Inversions .........................................................................93

    CHAPTER 12—Score Analysis ..........................................................................103

    SCORE ANALYSES ............................................................................................113

# 1 Fundamentals of Music: Pitch

Chapter 1 Review

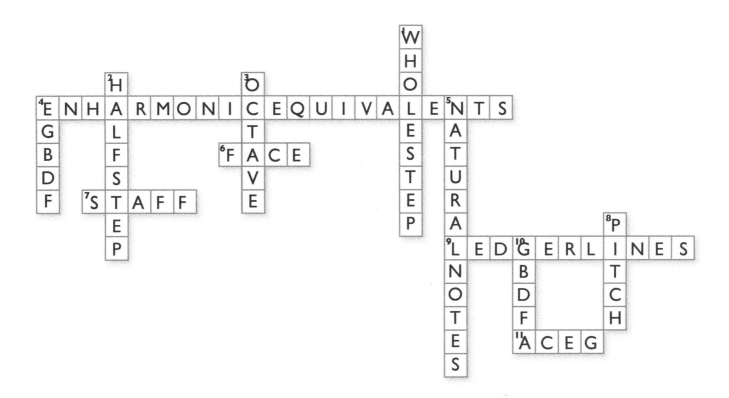

## Daily Exercises for Chapter 1

### ℬ EXERCISES FOR DAY 1

Re-read chapter 1 and complete the following exercises:

**Exercise 1.1**

Provide the letter names for each specified key marked on the keyboard.

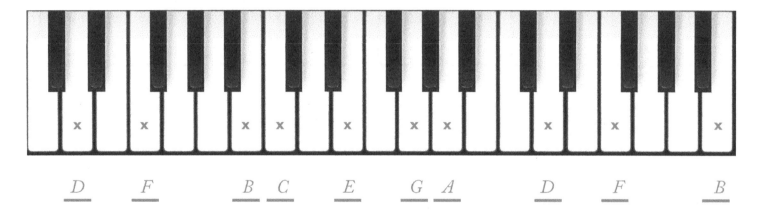

D    F        B    C    E    G    A        D    F        B

**Exercise 1.2**

Provide the name for each black key marked on the keyboard and include its enharmonic equivalent name.

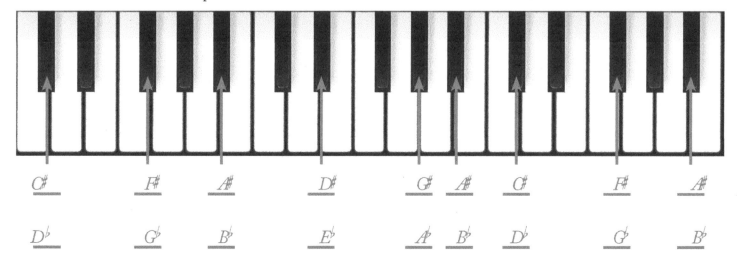

C♯        F♯    A♯        D♯        G♯    A♯    C♯        F♯    A♯

D♭        G♭    B♭        E♭        A♭    B♭    D♭        G♭    B♭

**Exercise 1.3**

Use arrows to show motions of whole or half steps above the given note.

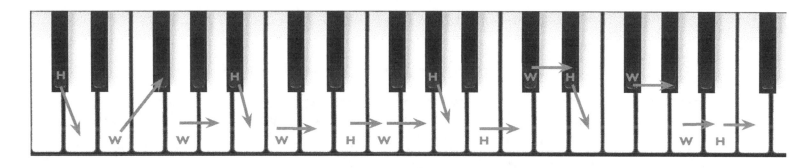

**Exercise 1.4**

On the staff below, write a flat in front of the first four notes, a sharp in front of the next four notes, and a natural in front of the final four notes.

**Exercise 1.5**

Give the note enharmonically equivalent to each of the following notes:

a) B♯ _C_  b) D♭ _C♯_  c) E♮ _F♭_  d) E♭ _D♯_

e) G♯ _A♭_  f) A♭ _G♯_  g) F♯ _G♭_  h) C♮ _B♯_

 EXERCISES FOR DAY 2

Re-read chapter 1 and complete the following exercises:

**Exercise 1.6**

Practice drawing the symbols for a treble and bass clef on the following staves (plural of "staff").

Bonus: Try using a calligraphy pen to achieve the broader and narrower sections of the lines.

**Exercise 1.7**

Name the following notes on the treble clef:

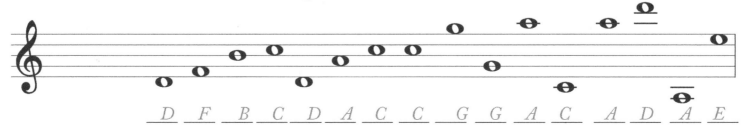

D  F  B  C  D  A  C  C  G  G  A  C  A  D  A  E

Name the following notes on the bass clef:

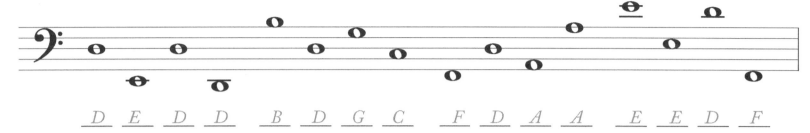

D  E  D  D  B  D  G  C  F  D  A  A  E  E  D  F

**Exercise 1.8**

Draw arrows from the treble clef set of notes to the correct key on the keyboard.

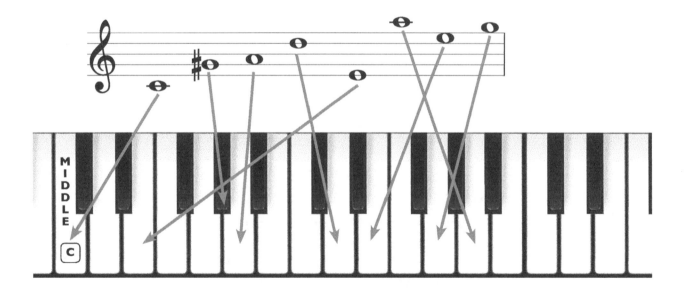

Draw arrows from the bass clef set of notes to the correct key on the keyboard.

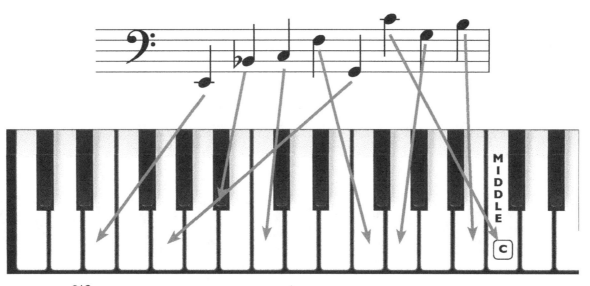

𝄢 EXERCISES FOR DAY 3

The figures in the following exercises are excerpts from the scores at the end of your book. Refer to the scores to guide you through these exercises.

**Exercise 1.9**

The following excerpt is the third line on the treble clef of the hymn "When Peace Like a River." Label these notes with the correct note names.

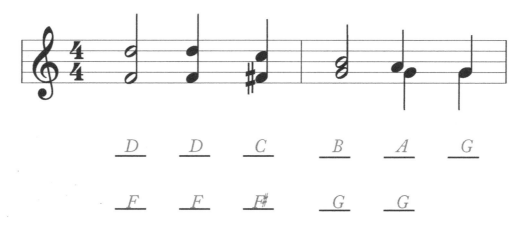

**Exercise 1.10**

The following excerpt is the third line on the bass clef of the hymn "When Peace Like a River." Identify the numbered notes by writing their numbers on the keyboard below.

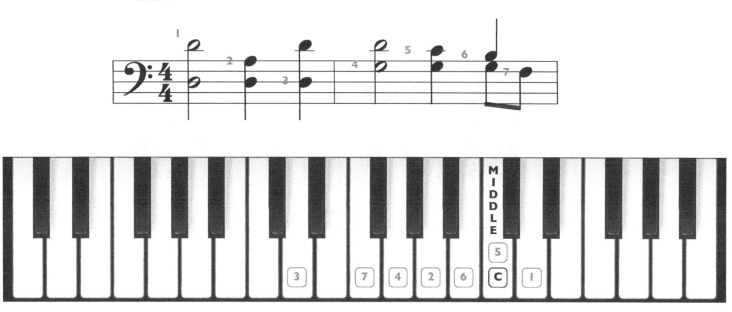

🎶 EXERCISES FOR DAY 4

**Exercise 1.11**

Write the following notes on the treble clef (there can be more than one correct answer). The first one is done for you with all possible answers.

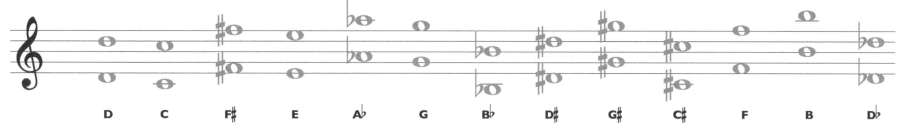

D    C    F#    E    A♭    G    B♭    D#    G#    C#    F    B    D♭

**Exercise 1.12**

Write the following notes on the bass clef:

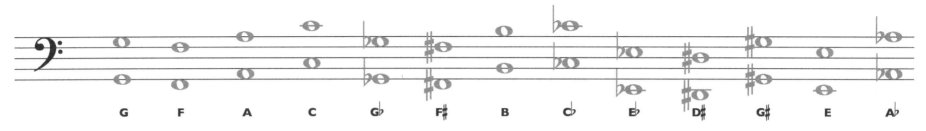

G    F    A    C    G♭    F♯    B    C♭    E♭    D♯    G♯    E    A♭

**Exercise 1.13**

Draw arrows from the notes on the staff to their corresponding keys on the keyboard (MC = middle C).

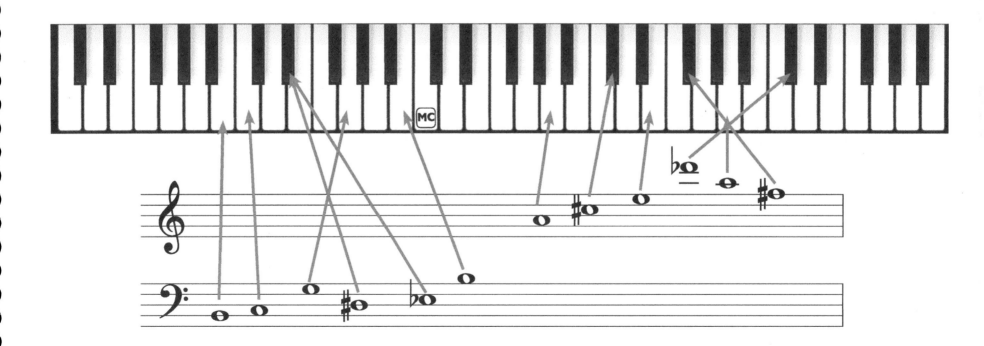

**Exercise 1.14**

Notate each note with an "x" on the staff provided below. Once notated, draw arrows from the keys on the keyboard to their corresponding notes on the staff (MC = middle C).

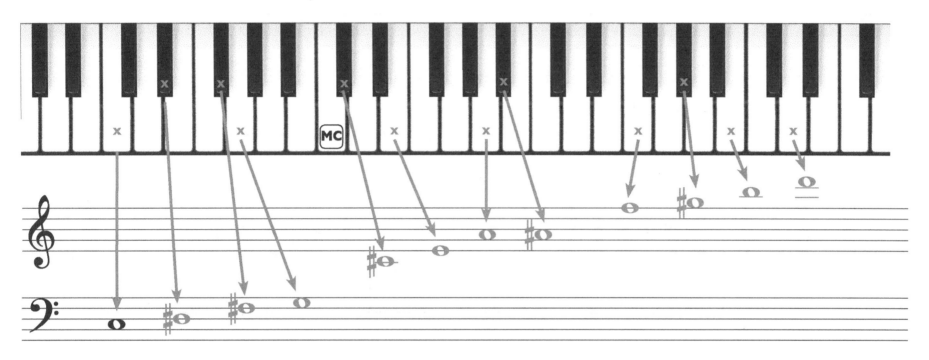

**or**

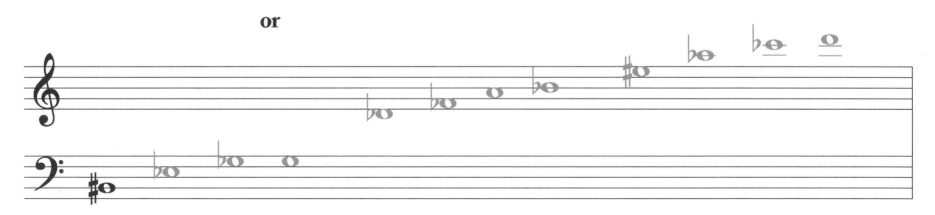

**Exercise 1.15**

Use the keyboard below to mark the following keys and specific octaves:

a)  Label all of the C keys on the keyboard with a C directly below each key.

b)  Label all of the F♯ keys on the keyboard with an F♯ directly above each key.

c)  Label all the G octaves on the keyboard with a G and the correct register designation on each key.

d)  Label all the E octaves on the keyboard with an E and the correct register designation on each key.

e)  Mark the keys on the keyboard that do not belong to any octave charts by writing an "x" on the keys.

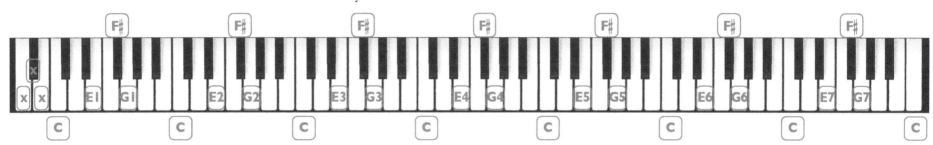

# 2 Introduction to Rhythm

## Chapter 2 Review

```
H A L F N O T E V D K R P U A E I T
F M R E S I K G U E W F H U F Q R S
F Q O G C K N U L E R W G Y M I H E
E H C U U L X T E T W M D S T S L T
W T I N F U W C C O E N X T H R S
Z G O E T O N H T N E E T X I S M E
C E C N F Q Q W T H W A P T W G T R
J N B G R A A A S T C N S Z J O Q R
L Z C Q Z F T V N H Y O O F N I F E
F E J H V I T L I G J F U E Y P G T
W W S T O N H R P I B W L P W V A R
H W H N B N E O A E W O P U Q N M A
A V D C M E H H O U H M G H F V J U
Q O P J V E J X Y W Q C K B V K E Q
T R C Y M E V Y Z N R Q I E U I X Q
X C J H V B R X K E A T A J Q B G
N R H P W B G P S H N Z F M A X H I
D R C Z F M P T S M J G E A P I S F
```

## Daily Exercises for Chapter 2

 EXERCISES FOR DAY 1

Read through chapter 2 and complete the following exercises:

**Exercise 2.1**

On the staff below write two whole notes, four half notes, and four quarter notes.
(The stem, if needed, can go either up or down.)

**Exercise 2.2**

On the staff below write six eighth notes with flags, three groupings of two eighth
notes beamed together, six sixteenth notes with flags, and three groupings of two
sixteenth notes beamed together. (The stem, if needed, can go either up or down.)

## 𝄢 EXERCISES FOR DAY 2

Review chapter 2 and complete the following exercises:

**Exercise 2.3**

Answer the following questions and prepare to do some math:

a)  How many half notes make up one whole note?     *2*

b)  How many quarter notes make up one half note?   *2*

c)  How many eighth notes make up one half note?       *4*

d)  How many sixteenth notes make up one whole note?   *16*

e)  How many sixteenth notes make up four eighth notes?   *8*

f)  How many eighth notes make up four half notes?   *16*

g)  How many quarter notes make up four whole notes?   *16*

h)  Thirty-two sixteenth notes make up how many whole notes?   *2*

i)  Sixteen quarter notes make up how many half notes?   *8*

j)  Thirty-two eighth notes make up how many half notes?   *8*

**Exercise 2.4**

Write a note equal to the following sets of notes.

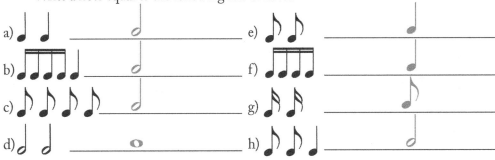

## 🎵 EXERCISES FOR DAY 3

Review chapter 2 and complete the following exercises:

**Exercise 2.5**

Write two notes whose combined value is equal to the following sets of notes:

*There are other possible answers than those shown here if dotted notes are used.*

**Exercise 2.6**

Draw the corresponding rest sign next to the following notes:

a) ♪ = ꞯ

d) ♬ = ꞯ

b) 𝅝 = ▬

e) 𝅗𝅥 = ▬

c) ♩ = 𝄽

**Exercise 2.7**

Draw a single rest equal to the following sets of notes:

a) ♬ ♩ = ▬

e) 𝅗𝅥 𝅗𝅥 = ▬

b) ♪ ♪ = 𝄽

f) ♩ ♬ 𝅗𝅥 = ▬

c) ♪ ♪ ♪ ♪ = ▬

g) ♩ ♩ = ▬

d) ♪ ♪ = ꞯ

h) ♪ ♪ ♩ = ▬

## ❦ EXERCISES FOR DAY 4

Review chapter 2 and complete the following exercises:

**Exercise 2.8**

Write two notes or rests whose combined value is equal to the following sets of dotted notes and rests. Use notes when notes are given; use rests when rests are given.

1. 𝅗𝅥. = ___ 𝅗𝅥 ___ + ___ 𝅘𝅥 ___

2. 𝅘𝅥. = ___ 𝅘𝅥 ___ + ___ 𝅘𝅥𝅮 ___

3. (rest) = ___ (rest) ___ + ___ (rest) ___

4. (rest) = ___ (rest) ___ + ___ (rest) ___

5. 𝅝. = ___ 𝅝 ___ + ___ 𝅗𝅥 ___

6. 𝅘𝅥𝅮. = ___ 𝅘𝅥𝅮 ___ + ___ 𝅘𝅥𝅯 ___

7. (rest). = ___ (rest) ___ + ___ (rest) ___

8. (rest). = ___ (rest) ___ + ___ (rest) ___

**Exercise 2.9**

Given the tied notes below, write a single note of equal value.

1.       =    ♩ (half note)

2.       =    𝅝 (whole note)

3.       =    ♩ (quarter note)

4.       =    𝅝 (whole note)

5.       =    𝅗𝅥. (dotted half note)

6.       =    ♪. (dotted eighth note)

# 3 Simple Meter

Chapter 3 Review

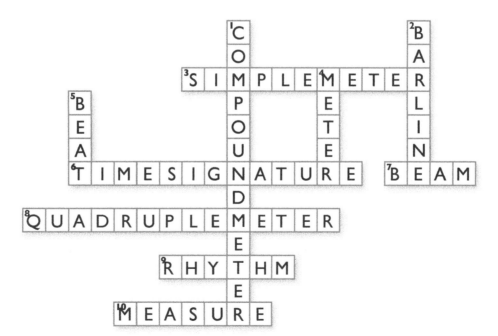

## Daily Exercises for Chapter 3

### ✵ EXERCISES FOR DAY 1

**Exercise 3.1**

Read through chapter 3 and answer the following questions:

a) What is a beat?
 *A beat is the fixed, rhythmic pulse of a piece of music.*

b) What is meter? *Meter is the specific beat groupings and divisions that occur
 within music.*

c) What is a bar line?
 *A vertical line that separates one measure from another on the staff.*

d) What is a measure?
 *A measure is a singular grouping of beats.*

e) What is a time signature? *The vertical stack of numbers placed at the beginning of the
 staff immediately following the clef to indicate the meter.*

**Exercise 3.2**

What type of meter (simple or compound) do the time signatures below represent?

(a) $\frac{6}{8}$ _____*compound*_____

(b) $\frac{4}{4}$ _____*simple*_____

(c) $\frac{2}{8}$ _____*simple*_____

(d) $\frac{9}{16}$ _____*compound*_____

(e) $\frac{12}{4}$ _____*compound*_____

(f) $\frac{3}{4}$ _____*simple*_____

## ✥ EXERCISES FOR DAY 2

**Exercise 3.3**

What does the top number of a time signature that represents simple meter communicate?

*The top number of a time signature represents the number of beats in each measure.*

What does the bottom number of a time signature that represents simple meter communicate?

*The bottom number of a time signature represents the type of note that represents the beat.*

**Exercise 3.4**

Complete the following using the excerpt below.

a) Using the appropriate numbers or syllables, write out the correct rhythm for
   the notes on the treble clef lines. The first measure has been done for you as an
   example.

b) Practice reading rhythm by counting or clapping the treble clef melody aloud.

## When I Survey the Wondrous Cross

LENT

*Words: Isaac Watts, 1707.*
*Music: 'Hamburg', Lowell Mason, 1824.  Setting: "Northfield Hymnal", 1904.*
*copyright: public domain.  This score is a part of the Open Hymnal Project, 2014 Revision.*

**BONUS**

**Remember: Always beam to the beat.**

🎕 EXERCISES FOR DAY 3

**Exercise 3.5**

Fill in the correct note values to complete the following measures so that they match the time signature. Be creative with combinations of notes that fit each time signature.

*Other combinations are possible.*

**Exercise 3.6**

On the staves provided, rewrite the given measures so that the notes are beamed correctly. Remember, beam to the beat.

**Exercise 3.7**

Identify the following time signatures as duple, triple, or quadruple.

(a) $\dfrac{2}{2}$   _duple_

(b) $\dfrac{3}{4}$   _triple_

(c) $\dfrac{4}{8}$   _quadruple_

(d) $\dfrac{2}{16}$   _duple_

(e) $\dfrac{4}{4}$   _quadruple_

🎵 EXERCISES FOR DAY 4

**Exercise 3.8**

Using numbers and the syllables "e," "&," and "a," count the exercises below. Make sure you know which note value gets the beat.

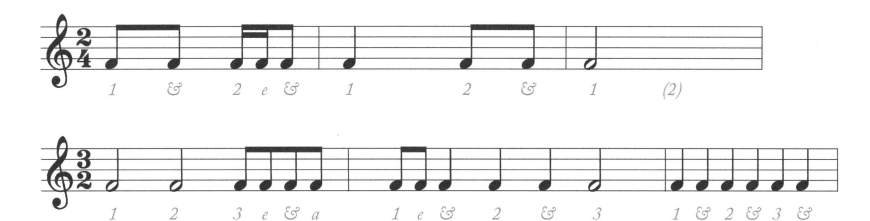

**Exercise 3.9**

Answer the following questions about the excerpt from "When Peace Like a River." The second musical line is given for extra practice.

a) Starting with the first *full* measure (beginning on the word "peace"), write out the rhythm of the top notes in the treble clef (the melody). The first note is shown as an example.

b) Practice reading rhythm by counting or clapping the treble clef melody aloud.

c) Label the name of each note (e.g., A, B, C, etc.) on this excerpt to the right of the note.

# 4 Compound Meter

## Chapter 4 Review

_d_ _____ 1. Compound meter

_f_ _____ 2. Dotted notes

_c_ _____ 3. Compound triple meter

_e_ _____ 4. Compound quadruple meter

_g_ _____ 5. Top number in compound meter

_a_ _____ 6. Bottom number in compound meter

_i_ _____ 7. Compound duple meter

_h_ _____ 8. Dotted quarter note

_b_ _____ 9. Dotted half note

a) The note value of the subdivisions of the beat

b) The note that gets the beat in $\frac{9}{4}$ compound meter

c) Three beats per measure

d) With this meter, the beat is always on a dotted note

e) Four beats per measure

f) Only these notes can be divided into three equal parts

g) The number of subdivisions of the beat in each measure

h) The note that gets the beat in $\frac{6}{8}$ compound meter

i) Two beats per measure

## Daily Exercises

 EXERCISES FOR DAY 1

**Exercise 4.1**

Read through Chapter 4 and answer the following questions:

1) How many subdivisions are in a beat of compound meter?   *3*

2) In compound time signatures, what does the top number mean?
   *Number of subdivisions of the beat per measure*

3) In compound time signatures, what does the bottom number mean?
   *Note value that receives the subdivisions of the beat*

4) In compound meter, how many beats do duple, triple, and quadruple meters have
   per measure?
   *duple = 2, triple = 3, and quadruple = 4*

**Exercise 4.2**

Fill in each measure below with notes that correspond to the requested time signature. Be creative with combinations of note values that fit each time signature.
*Answers will vary.*

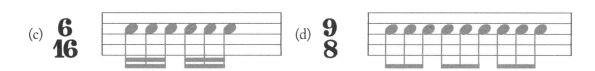

**Exercise 4.3**

Write the note value of the beat in each of the following compound time signatures:

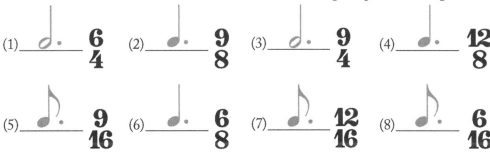

(1) _____ **6/4**    (2) _____ **9/8**    (3) _____ **9/4**    (4) _____ **12/8**

(5) _____ **9/16**    (6) _____ **6/8**    (7) _____ **12/16**    (8) _____ **6/16**

## EXERCISES FOR DAY 2

**Exercise 4.4**

The following excerpt is the first line from Bach's "Jesu, Joy of Man's Desiring." Use this excerpt to answer the questions below. You may want to find a recording online in order to listen to the piece and study the rhythm.

1) How many beats are in each measure? *3*

2) Which note value is getting the beat? *Dotted quarter note* (♩.)

3) Are the eighth notes in the treble clef beamed correctly? *Yes*

4) Why or why not? *They are beamed to the beat.*

**Exercise 4.5**

Match the simple and compound time signatures with the correct criteria (there may be more than one answer for each time signature).

1) _c g j_      $\frac{4}{4}$        a)  Duple meter

2) _b j h_      $\frac{3}{2}$        b)  Triple meter

3) _b h k e_      $\frac{9}{4}$        c)  Quadruple meter

4) _c k g_      $\frac{12}{8}$        d)  Beat value = ♪.

5) _a k h e_      $\frac{6}{4}$        e)  Beat value = 𝅗𝅥.

6) _b k g_      $\frac{9}{8}$        f)  Beat value = ♪

7) _b j i f_      $\frac{3}{8}$        g)  Subdivision(s) of beat = ♪

8) _c k i d_      $\frac{12}{16}$        h)  Subdivision(s) of beat = ♩

9) _a k i d_      $\frac{6}{16}$        i)  Subdivision(s) of beat = ♪

10) _a j h_      $\frac{2}{2}$        j)  Simple meter

                                                           k)  Compound meter

*…Thus much of music, which makes a fair ending; for what should be the end of music if not the love of beauty?*

—Plato

❧ EXERCISES FOR DAY 3

**Exercise 4.6**

Rewrite the following examples so that the notes are beamed correctly. Remember, beam notes to the beat.

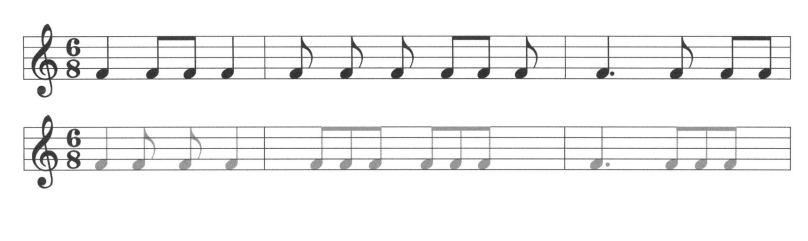

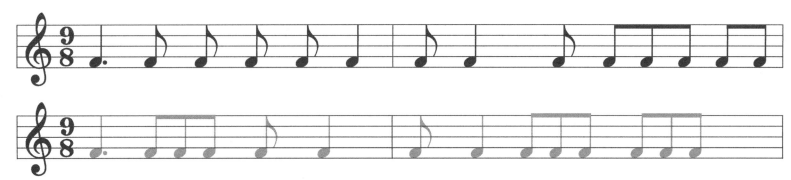

**⛧ EXERCISES FOR DAY 4**

**Exercise 4.7**

Match the correct time signature with the melodies below.

a) $\frac{6}{4}$     b) $\frac{9}{8}$     c) $\frac{3}{8}$     d) $\frac{6}{8}$     e) $\frac{4}{4}$

1. *b* _____

2. *c* _____

3. *a* _____

4. *e* _____

5. *d* _____

**Exercise 4.8**

Given the time signatures below, identify the meter type, the number of beats in each measure, and the note value that receives the beat.

| | Meter type | Beats/ measure | Note value |
|---|---|---|---|
| (a) **6/8** | *compound* | *2* | 𝅘𝅥𝅭 |
| (b) **4/4** | *simple* | *4* | 𝅘𝅥 |
| (c) **9/16** | *compound* | *3* | 𝅘𝅥𝅮𝅭 |
| (d) **12/16** | *compound* | *4* | 𝅘𝅥𝅮𝅭 |
| (e) **3/2** | *simple* | *3* | 𝅗𝅥 |
| (f) **2/8** | *simple* | *2* | 𝅘𝅥𝅮 |
| (g) **12/4** | *compound* | *4* | 𝅗𝅥𝅭 |

 # 5 Scales

## Chapters 1–5 Review

| | |
|---|---|
| _g_ | 1. ACEG |
| _j_ | 2. Augmentation dot |
| _l_ | 3. Beat |
| _r_ | 4. Bottom number in simple meter |
| _o_ | 5. Compound meter |
| _u_ | 6. D-E-F♯-G-A-B-C♯-D |
| _v_ | 7. D-E-F-G-A-B♭-C-D |
| _d_ | 8. EGBDF |
| _c_ | 9. Enharmonic equivalent |
| _e_ | 10. FACE |
| _f_ | 11. GBDFA |
| _a_ | 12. Half step |
| _m_ | 13. Meter |
| _i_ | 14. Quarter note |
| _n_ | 15. Simple meter |
| _k_ | 16. Tie |
| _p_ | 17. Time signature |
| _q_ | 18. Top number in simple meter |
| _h_ | 19. Whole note |
| _b_ | 20. Whole step |
| _t_ | 21. W-H-W-W-H-W-W |
| _s_ | 22. W-W-H-W-W-W-H |

a. The shortest distance between two notes

b. The distance of pitch equal to two half steps

c. Two notes that have the same pitch but different names

d. Notation on the staff lines in a treble clef

e. Notation in the spaces of the staff in a treble clef

f. Notation on the staff lines in a bass clef

g. Notation in the spaces of the staff in a bass clef

h. Twice the value of a half note

i. Twice the value of an eighth note

j. Increases the note value of a note or rest by half the value of the note or rest

k. Used to add the lengths of two notes together to prolong the pitch

l. The fixed, rhythmic pulse of a piece of music

m. The specific beat groupings and divisions that occur within the music

n. Meter in which the beat is divided into two equal parts

o. Meter in which the beat is divided into three equal parts

p. A vertical stack of numbers placed at the beginning of the staff immediately following the clef that indicates the meter

q. Denotes how many beats there are per measure

r. Denotes which type of note serves as the beat

s. The pattern of whole and half steps in a major scale

t. The pattern of whole and half steps in a natural minor scale

u. D major scale

v. D minor scale

## Daily Exercises for Chapter 5

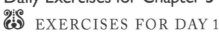 EXERCISES FOR DAY 1

**Exercise 5.1**

Read through chapter 5 and answer the following questions:

a) What is a scale? *A scale is a series of musical notes organized by ascending or descending pitches.*

b) If both the major and minor scales contain eight notes, what is the difference between major and minor scales?
*the whole- and half-step patterns*

c) What is the pattern of whole steps and half steps for major scales?
*W–W–H–W–W–W–H*

d) What is the pattern of whole steps and half steps for natural minor scales?
*W–H–W–W–H–W–W*

e) What is the term for the distance between two notes with the same name?
*octave*

**Exercise 5.2**

Practice recognizing whole steps and half steps on a staff by labeling the following distances between the pairs of notes in each measure as either a whole step or a half step.

1.

_____ *H* _____    _____ *W* _____    _____ *H* _____    _____ *H* _____    _____ *H* _____

**2.** Write your own pairs of notes with the indicated half step or whole step. Use sharps and flats, if needed. *Answers will vary.*

**whole step**          **half step**          **whole step**          **whole step**          **half step**

**Exercise 5.3**

Fill in the missing notes to the scales given below by notating them on the staff.

Label each note you just notated as either a whole or half step from the note before it.

## ⚜ EXERCISES FOR DAY 2

**Exercise 5.4**

Fill in the missing notes in the following major scales. Use the keyboard sheet in the Helpful Tools section if you need to.

1.   D     E     *F♯*     G     *A*     *B*     C♯     D

2.   A     B     C♯     *D*     E     *F♯*    *G♯*     A

3.  *G*     A     B     C     *D*     *E*     F♯     G

4.   B♭    *C*     D     *E♭*    *F*     G     A     B♭

5.   F     G     *A*    *B♭*     C     D     *E*     F

6.   E     F♯    *G♯*     A     *B*     C♯    *D♯*     E

Take two scales from above and notate the scales on the staves below. Notate the scales in ascending and descending order, with one scale in the treble clef and one in the bass clef. If there are sharps or flats, place them to the left of the note.

**Exercise 5.5**

Use the major and minor scale patterns of whole steps and half steps to answer the questions below. You may find it helpful to use the keyboard sheet in the Helpful Tools section.

a)  How many sharps are in the D major scale?  *2*

b)  How many flats are in the E♭ major scale?  *3*

c)  How many flats are in the C natural minor scale?  *3*

d)  How many sharps are in the F♯ natural minor scale?  *3*

### EXERCISES FOR DAY 3

**Exercise 5.6**

In each example, the first note of the scale is given. Notate the indicated ascending and descending major scale. Use sharps and flats to the left of the note if needed.  Note: Once a sharp or flat appears, it is assumed that it applies through the end of the measure unless notated otherwise.

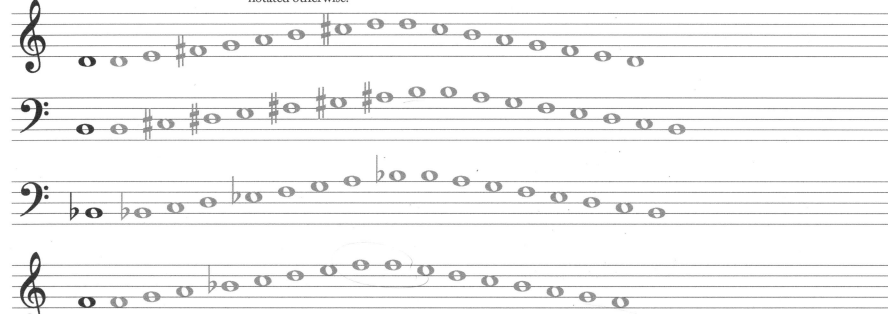

**Exercise 5.7**

In each example, the first note of the scale is given. Notate the indicated ascending and descending natural minor scale. Use sharps and flats to the left of the note if needed.

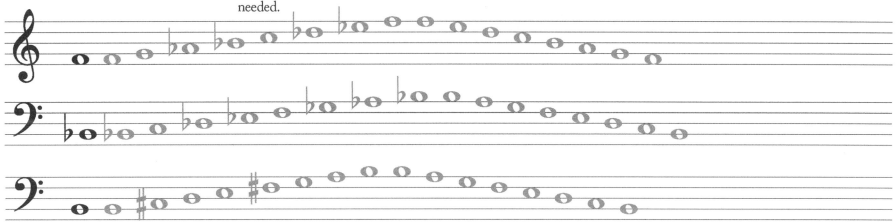

## ❧ EXERCISES FOR DAY 4

**Exercise 5.8**

a) Write a melody in the following blank measures using only the notes that are part of the E major scale. You will need to add sharps or flats to specific notes.

*Make sure that each measure contains note values that add up to three quarter notes and that the melody uses only the notes from the E major scale.*

b) Write a melody in the following blank measures using only the notes that are part of the A♭ major scale. You will need to add sharps or flats to specific notes.

*Make sure that each measure contains note values that add up to two half notes and that the melody uses only the notes from the A♭ major scale.*

**Exercise 5.9**

Identify the following major or natural minor scales. Remember, descending scales use the pattern backwards. It might be helpful to label whole steps and half steps on the scale so you can identify major or minor correctly.

**1.** *B natural minor scale*

**2.** *E major scale*

**3.** *A major scale*

**4.** *G major scale*

**5.** *D natural minor scale*

**6.** *Bb major scale*

# 6 Key Signatures

## Chapter 6 Review

Some questions may have more than one answer.

_____j_____    1. Indicates the key of the piece at the beginning of the staff by showing which sharps or flats are to be used

      a. A major

_____f_____    2. Order of sharps that appears in key signatures from left to right

      b. B E A D G C F

_____b_____    3. Order of flats that appears in key signatures from left to right

      c. B major

      d. D minor

_____k_____    4. Pairs of major and minor scales that share the same key signature

      e. Enharmonic equivalent key signatures

_____e_____    5. The key of F♯ major and G♭ major are said to be this.

      f. F C G D A E B

      g. F major

_____a, h_____    6. Key signature with three sharps

      h. F♯ minor

_____c, i_____    7. Key signature with five sharps

      i. G♯ minor

      j. Key signature

_____g, d_____    8. Key signature with one flat

      k. Relative keys

## Daily Exercises for Chapter 6

❦ EXERCISES FOR DAY 1

**Exercise 6.1**

Read through chapter 6 and answer the following questions. Draw your own circle of fifths diagram on a piece of scrap paper for practice.

a)  How many key signatures are in our Western style of music?

*15*

b)  What is a musical key?

*A specific set of pitches used to create a piece of music; the scale around which the music is centered.*

c)  In the Circle of Fifths diagram, starting on C major, which direction do the key signatures with sharps move? Which direction do the key signatures with flats move?

*clockwise; counterclockwise*

d)  What are enharmonic keys? Give an example, including the notes in the keys.

*Two scales with the same sounding notes that can be called by two different names.*

*Examples:*

*D flat major (D♭ E♭ F G♭ A♭ B♭ C) and C sharp major (C♯ D♯ E♯ F♯ G♯ A♯ B♯)*

*F sharp major (F♯ G♯ A♯ B C♯ D♯ E♯) and G flat major (G♭ A♭ B♭ C♭ D♭ E♭ F)*

*B major (B C♯ D♯ E F♯ G♯ A♯) and C flat major (C♭ D♭ E♭ F♭ G♭ B♭)*

*G sharp minor (G♯ A♯ B C♯ D♯ E F♯) and A flat minor (A♭ B♭ C♭ D♭ E♭ F♭ G♭)*

*D sharp minor (D♯ E♯ F♯ G♯ A♯ B C♯) and E flat minor (E♭ F G♭ A♭ B♭ C♭ D♭)*

*A sharp minor (A♯ B♯ C♯ D♯ E♯ F♯ G♯) and B flat minor (B♭ C D♭ E♭ F G♭ A♭)*

## EXERCISES FOR DAY 2

**Exercise 6.2**

Practice drawing your own circle of fifths diagram on scrap paper.

On the staves below and on the next page, write the indicated major key signature. Be sure to provide the correct order of sharps or flats within the key signature.

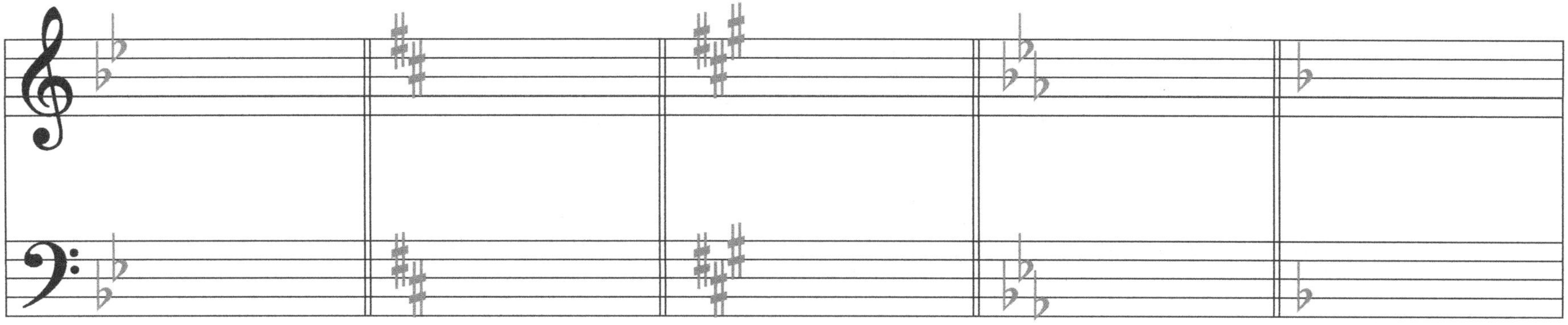

B♭ D A E♭ F

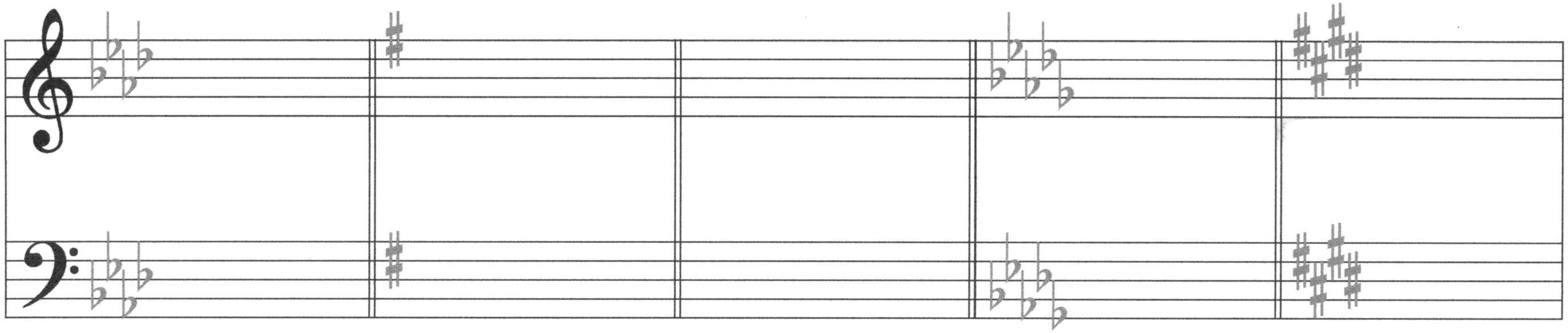

A♭ G C D♭ E

❧ EXERCISES FOR DAY 3

**Exercise 6.3**

Use the first line excerpt below from the hymn "Be Thou My Vision" to answer the questions below.

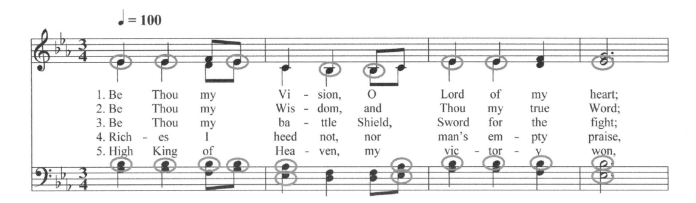

a)  What major key is the piece above in? *E♭ major*

b)  Which notes are flatted in the key signature above? *B, E, A*

c)  Which note value gets the beat? How many beats are in each measure?
    *quarter note; 3 beats in each measure*

d)  Circle all the notes in the piece in both the treble and bass clefs that are flats (key signature will help).

e)  In the second measure, treble clef, is there a whole step or half step step between the first two notes? *W*

**Exercise 6.4**

Use the first line excerpt below from the hymn "When I Survey the Wondrous Cross" to answer the questions below.

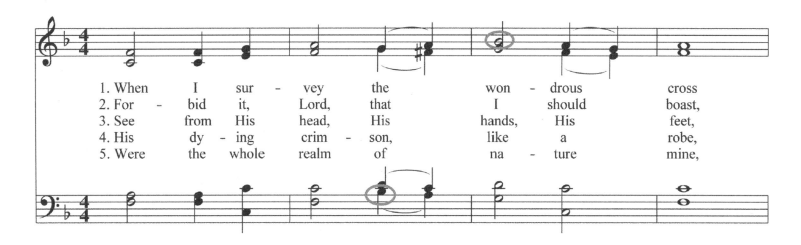

1. When      I      sur  –  vey      the              won  –  drous              cross
2. For  –  bid    it,      Lord,    that              I        should              boast,
3. See      from   His     head,    His              hands,   His                feet,
4. His      dy  – ing     crim  –  son,              like     a                  robe,
5. Were     the    whole   realm    of               na  –  ture              mine,

a) What major key is the excerpt above in? *F major*

b) What are the notes of the scale in the key above?
   *F–G–A–B♭–C–D–E–F*

c) Circle all the notes in the piece in both the treble and bass clefs that are flats (key signature will help).

d) Which note in this first line is not in the key signature of the piece? How do you know it is not in the key? *F♯; the key is F major, which does not contain an F♯. We also know because the sharp is present.*

e) Using the Circle of Fifths chart, which key going counterclockwise is after the key in this piece? How many flats or sharps are in this next key?
   *B♭ major; two flats*

**Exercise 6.5**

Using the techniques discussed in chapter 6, match the relative keys.

| | | |
|---|---|---|
| 1. __c__ D minor | | a) B♭ major |
| 2. __f__ C major | | b) G major |
| 3. __b__ E minor | | c) F major |
| 4. __e__ A major | | d) B minor |
| 5. __a__ G minor | | e) F♯ minor |
| 6. __d__ D major | | f) A minor |

## EXERCISES FOR DAY 4

**Exercise 6.6**

On the staves below and on the next page, write the indicated minor key signature. Be sure to provide the correct order of sharps or flats within the key signature. It may be helpful to find the relative major key first in order to write the correct key signature for each minor key.

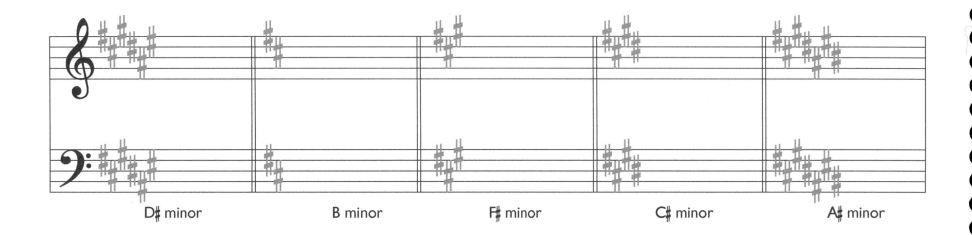

D♯ minor      B minor      F♯ minor      C♯ minor      A♯ minor

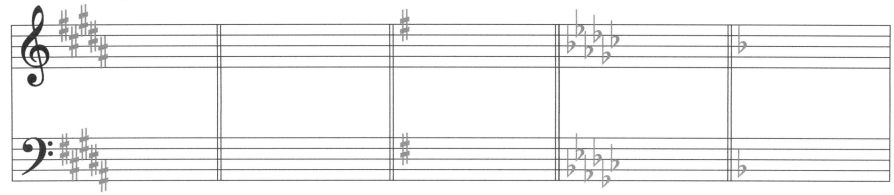

Exercise 6.7

Match the following key signatures to the correct key.

a) A minor     b) C♯ major     c) C minor     d) E major     e) D♭ major     f) C♭ major

g) D♯ minor     h) G♭ major     i) B minor     j) B major

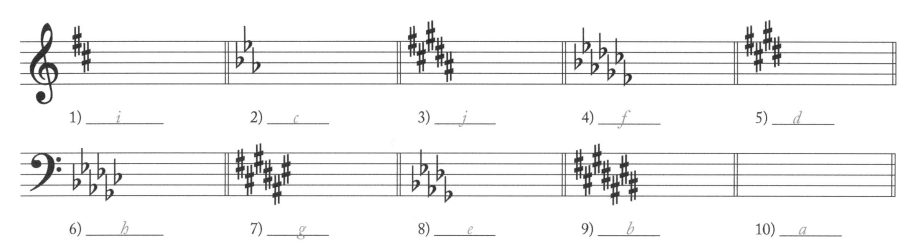

# 7 Scale Degrees and Transposition

Chapter 7 Review

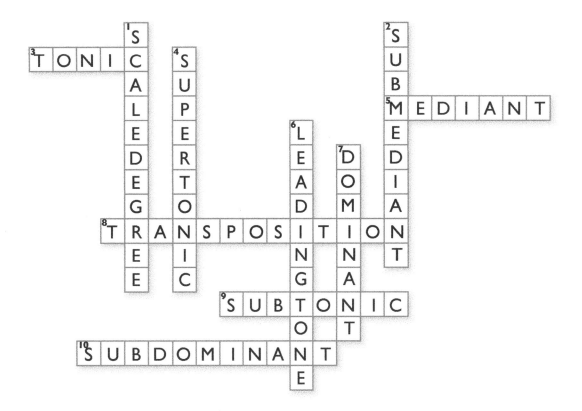

## Daily Exercises for Chapter 7
### ✣ EXERCISES FOR DAY 1

**Exercise 7.1**

Identify the major key and scale degree numbers for the following excerpts.

1) Bass of "Jesu, Joy of Man's Desiring"

Key: _G major_

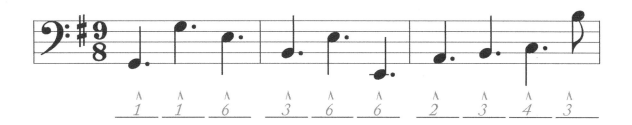

2) First line of "When I Survey the Wondrous Cross"

Key: _F major_

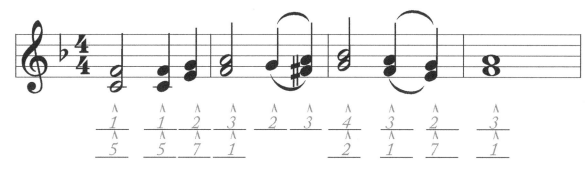

3) First line of "Be Thou My Vision"

Key: *Eb major*

♩ = 100

| 1. Be | Thou | my | Vi | - | sion, | O | | Lord | of | my | heart; |

∧ 1 ∧ 1 ∧ 2 ∧ 1 ∧ 6 ∧ 5 ∧ 5 ∧ 6 ∧ 1 ∧ 1 ∧ 2 ∧ 3

∧ 7      ∧ 7  ∧ 1

## ✺ EXERCISES FOR DAY 2

**Exercise 7.2**

Identify the major key and then write the correct note on the staff from the given scale degree name.

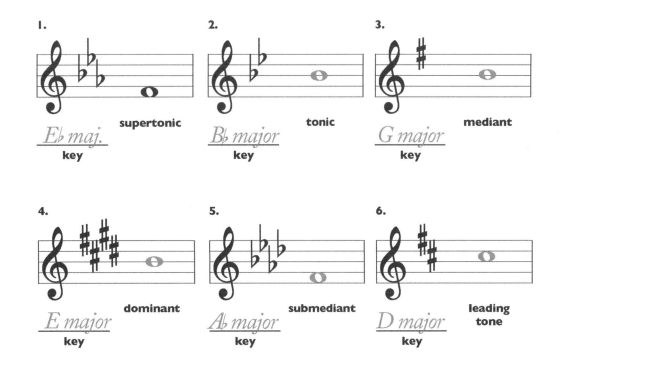

1.    supertonic    *Eb maj.*    key

2.    tonic    *Bb major*    key

3.    mediant    *G major*    key

4.    dominant    *E major*    key

5.    submediant    *Ab major*    key

6.    leading tone    *D major*    key

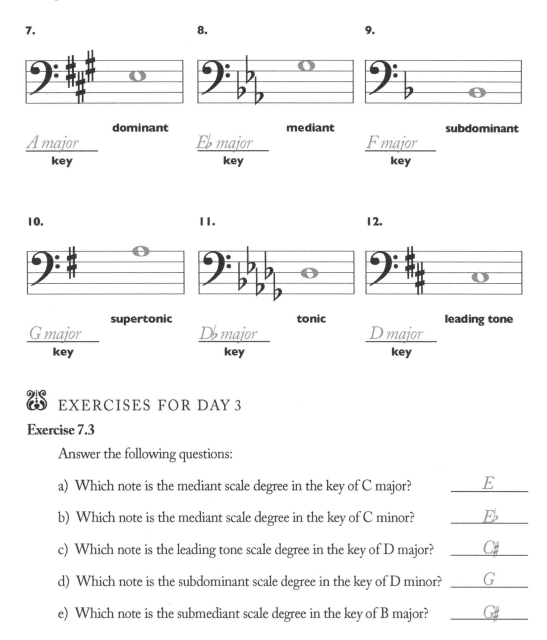

**7.**

**dominant**

*A major*

**key**

**8.**

**mediant**

*E♭ major*

**key**

**9.**

**subdominant**

*F major*

**key**

**10.**

**supertonic**

*G major*

**key**

**11.**

**tonic**

*D♭ major*

**key**

**12.**

**leading tone**

*D major*

**key**

## EXERCISES FOR DAY 3

**Exercise 7.3**

Answer the following questions:

a) Which note is the mediant scale degree in the key of C major?        *E*

b) Which note is the mediant scale degree in the key of C minor?        *E♭*

c) Which note is the leading tone scale degree in the key of D major?        *C♯*

d) Which note is the subdominant scale degree in the key of D minor?        *G*

e) Which note is the submediant scale degree in the key of B major?        *G♯*

**Exercise 7.4**

Transpose the following melodies into the indicated keys:

**1. major key of** *F major*

**key of G major**

**2. major key of** *D major*

**key of C major**

Using the blank staff below, compose a melody that fits the time signature.

**3. key of B♭**

*Each measure should contain notes whose values add up to four quarter notes.*

Now transpose your melody above to the key of A major.

*The first note of this melody should be one half step down from the first note of the melody in the key of B♭ major above. The rest of the notes should contain the corresponding distance of the notes in the key of B♭ major.*

❧ EXERCISES FOR DAY 4

**Exercise 7.5**

Identify the correct scale degree name for the circled notes in the excerpt from "Be Thou My Vision."

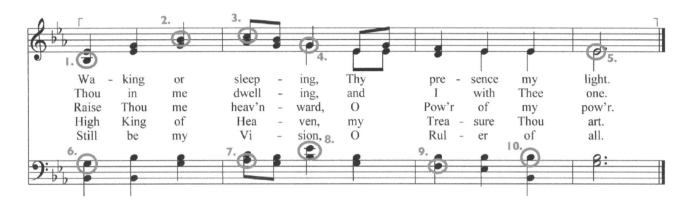

major key: ___E♭ major___

1) ___dominant___          6) ___mediant___

2) ___dominant___          7) ___subdominant___

3) ___submediant___        8) ___tonic___

4) ___mediant___           9) ___supertonic___

5) ___tonic___            10) ___dominant___

**Exercise 7.6**

Transpose the first line of the hymn "There Is a Fountain" into the key of C major. Remember that transposition only changes the pitch; it does not adjust the time signature or rhythm.

# There Is a Fountain

ZECHARIAH 13:1
William Cowper, *pub.*1772

CLEANSING FOUNTAIN
*attr. to* Lowell Mason

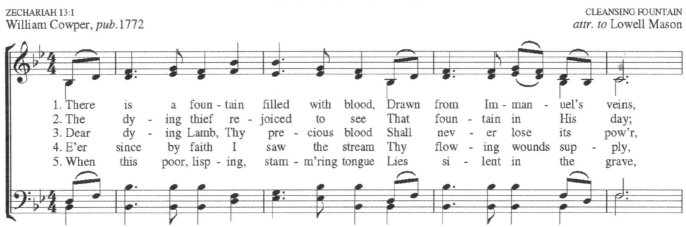

1. There        is        a  foun - tain    filled    with   blood,  Drawn   from    Im - man - uel's     veins,
2. The        dy - ing thief re - joiced    to      see    That    foun - tain  in      His      day;
3. Dear       dy - ing Lamb, Thy    pre - cious blood  Shall    nev - er    lose    its      pow'r,
4. E'er       since     by faith   I      saw    the   stream  Thy    flow - ing  wounds sup - ply,
5. When      this    poor, lisp - ing,   stam - m'ring tongue Lies     si - lent   in      the     grave,

# 8 Intervals

## Chapter 8 Review

_____e_____ 1. Interval

_____h_____ 2. Harmonic interval

_____c_____ 3. Melodic interval

_____f_____ 4. Interval size

_____b_____ 5. Interval quality

_____g_____ 6. Augmented

_____n_____ 7. Diminished

_____m_____ 8. Simple interval

_____k_____ 9. Compound interval

_____a_____ 10. Major sixth

_____j_____ 11. Minor sixth

_____p_____ 12. Perfect fourth

_____o_____ 13. Perfect fifth

_____l_____ 14. Diminished fifth

_____d_____ 15. Natural interval

_____i_____ 16. Adjusted interval

a. C–A interval quality

b. Denotes the specific type of relationship between two notes

c. When one note occurs after another note

d. An interval that is a natural part of a major scale

e. The distance between two notes or two pitches

f. The number of of lines and spaces, or letter names, represented on the staff

g. A major or perfect interval that has been raised by a half step

h. When two notes are played at the same time

i. An interval that occurs when the higher note is outside of the key or scale of the lower note

j. E–C quality interval

k. An interval with a size greater than an octave

l. C–G♭ quality interval

m. An interval within an octave of the starting pitch

n. A perfect or minor interval that has been lowered by a half step

o. F–C interval quality

p. C–F interval quality

## Daily Exercises for Chapter 8

 EXERCISES FOR DAY 1

### Exercise 8.1

Read through chapter 8 and answer the following questions:

a) What is an interval?

*An interval is the distance between two notes or two pitches.*

b) What is the difference between interval size and interval quality?

*Interval size is the number of lines and spaces, or letter names, represented on the staff. Interval quality is the specific type of relationship between two notes.*

c) What is the difference between harmonic and melodic intervals?

*When two notes are played at the same time, it is called a harmonic interval. When one note occurs after another note, it is called a melodic interval.*

d) What is the difference between simple and compound intervals?

*A simple interval is an interval within an octave of the starting pitch. A compound interval is an interval with a size of more than an octave.*

e) What prior knowledge of music theory is important for determining interval qualities?

*Knowledge of major scales and key signatures is important for determining interval qualities.*

**Exercise 8.2**

Use the measures below to answer the questions that follow.

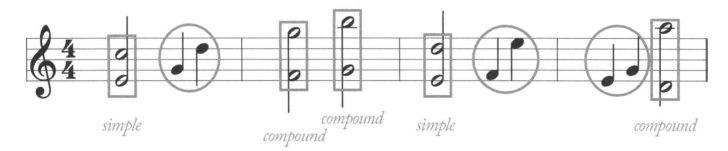

a) Circle the melodic intervals in the measures above.

b) Place a box around the harmonic intervals in the measures above.

c) Label the harmonic intervals that are also simple intervals.

d) Label the harmonic intervals that are also compound intervals.

## ⚬ EXERCISES FOR DAY 2

**Exercise 8.3**

Identify the size of the intervals below.

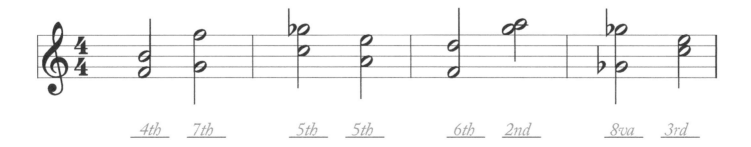

**Exercise 8.4**

Identify the following intervals including size and quality. Remember to use the key
of the lowest note even if it differs from the given key signature.

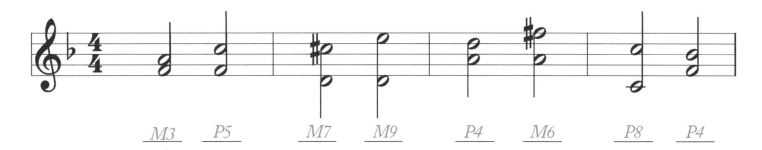

M3        P5        M7        M9        P4        M6        P8        P4

## 🎵 EXERCISES FOR DAY 3

**Exercise 8.5**

Identify the following intervals as minor or major third intervals (M3 or m3).
Remember to use the key signature of the lower note.

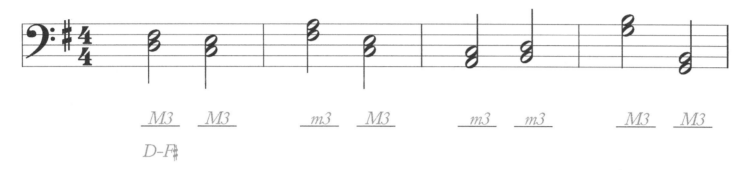

M3  M3   m3  M3   m3  m3   M3  M3

D-F♯

Identify the following intervals as minor or major sixth intervals (m6 or M6). Remember to use the key signature of the lower note.

M6  m6      M6  m6

**Exercise 8.6**

Identify the following intervals as minor or major seventh intervals. Remember to use the key signature of the lower note.

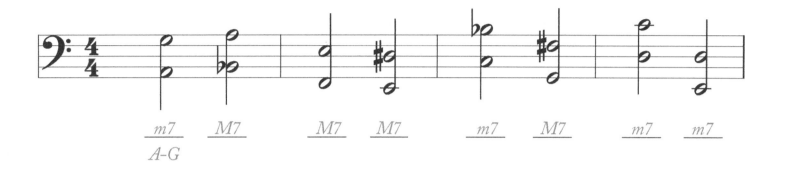

_m7_    _M7_        _M7_    _M7_        _m7_    _M7_        _m7_    _m7_

_A–G_

Identify the following intervals as perfect, augmented, or diminished fifths (P5) or fourths (P4). Remember to use the key signature of the lower note.

_A5_    _P5_                _P4_    _d5_

## ❧ EXERCISES FOR DAY 4

**Exercise 8.7**

Identify the following intervals below by quality. Remember, even though a key signature is given, you must always use the key of the lower note.

**Excerpt of the first line from "When I Survey the Wondrous Cross"**

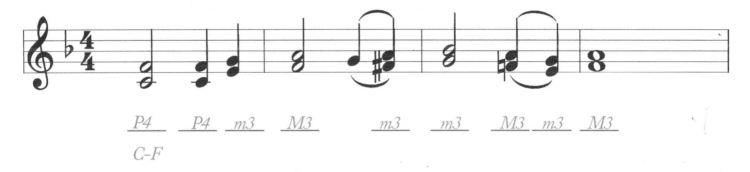

<u>P4</u>　<u>P4</u>　<u>m3</u>　<u>M3</u>　　<u>m3</u>　<u>m3</u>　<u>M3</u>　<u>m3</u>　<u>M3</u>

C-F

**Excerpt of the treble clef from the last line of "There Is a Fountain"**

<u>m6</u>　<u>M6</u>　　<u>M6</u>　<u>m6</u>　<u>M6</u>　<u>M6</u>　　<u>P5</u>　　<u>m3</u>　<u>M3</u>

D-B♭　　　　　　　　　　　　　　　　　　　　*melodic*

**Exercise 8.8**

Identify the following melodic intervals below by quality. Remember, even though a key signature is given, you must always use the key of the lower note.

**Excerpt of the bass clef from the first line of "Jesu, Joy of Man's Desiring"**

Hint: Always start with
the lower note, E–G

  P 8     m3     P4     P4     P8     P4     M2     m2

G2–G3

# 9 Triads and Triad Qualities

Chapter 9 Review

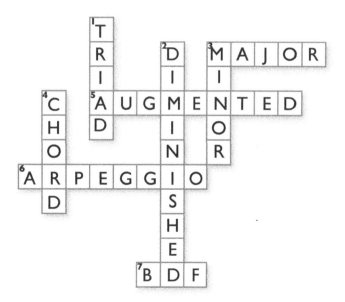

## Daily Exercises for Chapter 9

### ❧ EXERCISES FOR DAY 1

**Exercise 9.1**

Read through chapter 9 and answer the following questions:

a) What is the difference between a chord and a triad?

*A chord is a harmonious group of notes. A triad is a three-note chord consisting of the root, third, and fifth.*

b) What is an arpeggio?

*When the notes of a chord are broken up and played one after the other in sequence, they are called an arpeggio.*

c) What are the four qualities of triads?

*Major, minor, augmented, and diminished*

d) Give the symbols of the four qualities of triads. Use G as the root in your examples.

*G (major), Gm (minor), G+ (augmented), G∘ (diminished)*

e) Give the qualities of the intervals included in a major triad.

*major third and perfect fifth*

f) Give the qualities of the intervals included in a minor triad.

*minor third and perfect fifth*

**Exercise 9.2**

Supply the missing note in each triad to complete each of the triads below. Pay close attention to the quality indicated.

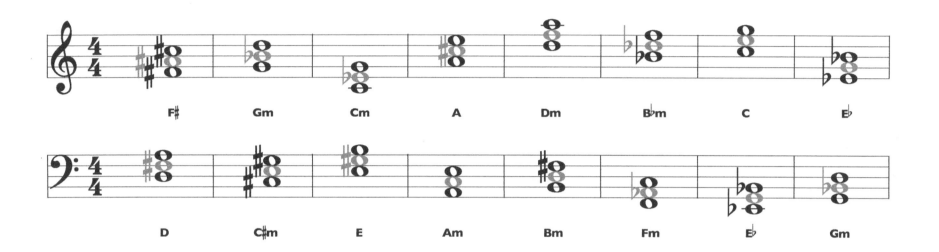

EXERCISES FOR DAY 2

**Exercise 9.3**

Supply the missing note (fifth) in each triad to complete each of the triads below. Pay close attention to the quality indicated.

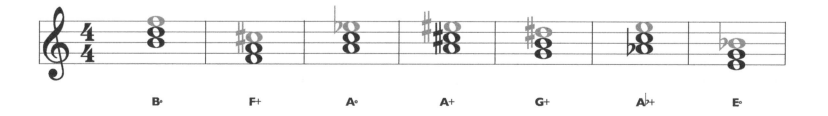

**Exercise 9.4**

Finish the indicated quality triads below.

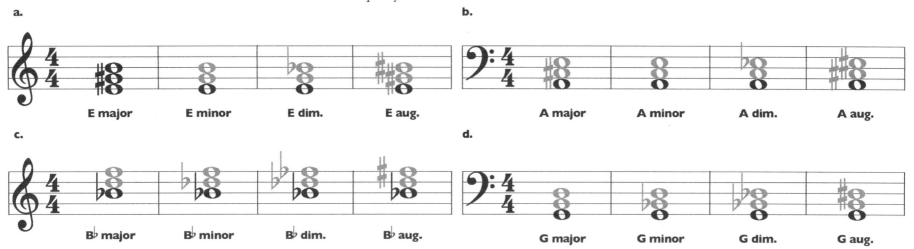

**Exercise 9.5**

Identify the quality of the triads below as major, minor, diminished, or augmented by using the root and correct chord symbol.

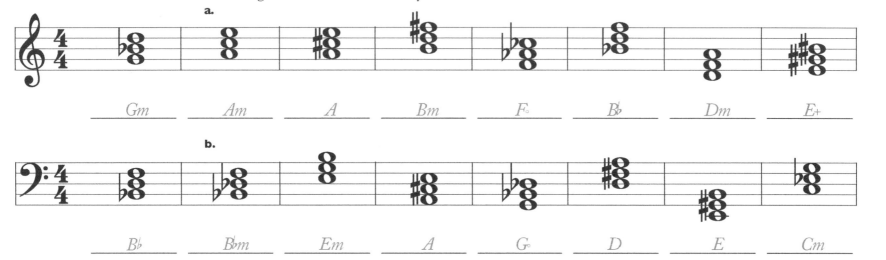

🎼 EXERCISES FOR DAY 3

**Exercise 9.6**

Correctly add sharps or flats to complete the requested qualities of the triads below.

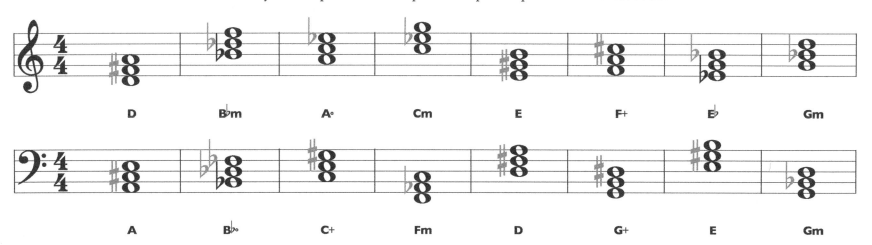

**Exercise 9.7**

Supply the missing notes to complete each of the triads below. Pay close attention to the quality indicated. The given note is the root.

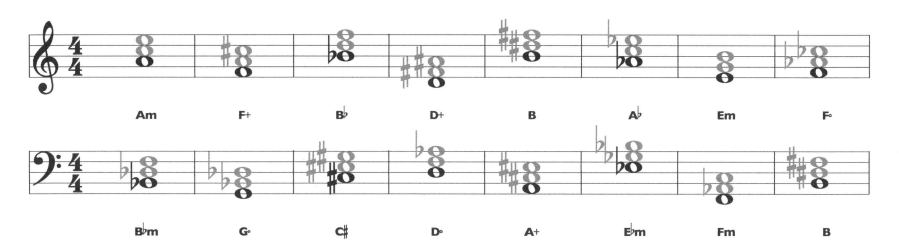

❧ EXERCISES FOR DAY 4

**Exercise 9.8**

Supply the missing notes to complete each of the triads below. Pay close attention to the quality indicated. The given note is the fifth, not the root. The first one is done for you.

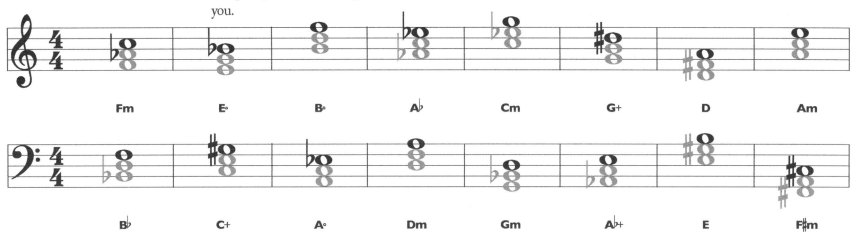

**Exercise 9.9**

Supply the missing notes to complete each of the triads below. For each triad, you are given a note, its position within the triad, and the triad quality. The first one is done for you.

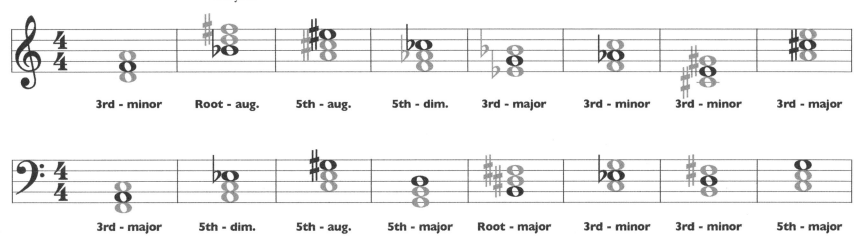

# 10 Triads: Roman Numeral Analysis

## Chapter 10 Review

Fill in the correct answers below.

_h_   1. ii

_a_   2. vi

_j_   3. III

_n_   4. V

_c_   5. iii

_i_   6. VI

_e_   7. IV

_m_   8. I

_f_   9. v

_d_   10. VII

_k_   11. vii°

_g_   12. ii°

_l_   13. i

_b_   14. iv

a. Submediant in major
b. Subdominant in minor
c. Mediant in major
d. Subtonic
e. Subdominant in major
f. Dominant in minor
g. Supertonic in minor
h. Supertonic in major
i. Submediant in minor
j. Mediant in minor
k. Leading tone
l. Tonic in minor
m. Tonic in major
n. Dominant in major

## Daily Exercises for Chapter 10

### ❧ EXERCISES FOR DAY 1

**Exercise 10.1**

Read through chapter 10 and answer the following questions:

a) What are diatonic triads?

> *Diatonic triads are triads that use only the notes, including sharps or flats, of a given scale.*

b) Why is analysis with Roman numerals helpful?

> *1. Roman numerals are used to communicate scale degree numbers and scale degree names.*
>
> *2. Roman numerals are used to communicate the quality of the triad.*
>
> *3. Roman numerals can be easily adjusted to communicate notes or chords outside the key.*

c) Give an example of an arpeggiated triad below, including a key signature and a bass or treble clef. *Answers will vary.*

**Exercise 10.2**

Label the triads below with the correct triad degrees, making sure to note the major key signatures.

**a.**

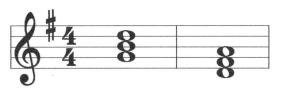

_tonic_        _dominant_

**b.**

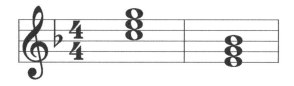

_dominant_        _leading tone_

**c.**

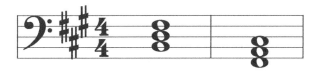

_supertonic_        _submediant_

**d.**

_mediant_        _supertonic_

❧ EXERCISES FOR DAY 2

**Exercise 10.3**

Give the corresponding Roman numeral, including quality, for the triad degrees below.

**Major Key**

a) supertonic: _____*ii*_____ b) dominant: _____*V*_____ c) submediant: _____*vi*_____

d) leading tone: _*vii°*_ e) mediant: _____*iii*_____ f) subdominant: _____*IV*_____

**Minor Key**

a) supertonic: _____*ii°*_____ b) dominant: _____*v*_____ c) submediant: _____*VI*_____

d) subtonic: _____*VII*_____ e) mediant: _____*III*_____ f) subdominant: _____*iv*_____

**Exercise 10.4**

Use Roman numerals to identify the triads in the indicated **major** keys.

**a.**

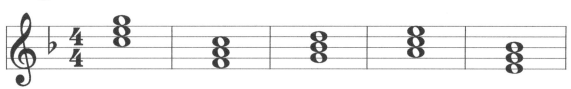

**F major**     *V*       *I*       *ii*       *iii*       *vii°*

**b.**

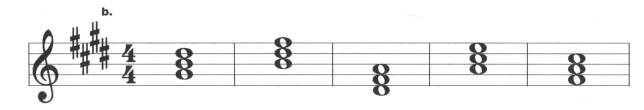

**E major**     *iii*       *V*       *vii°*       *IV*       *ii*

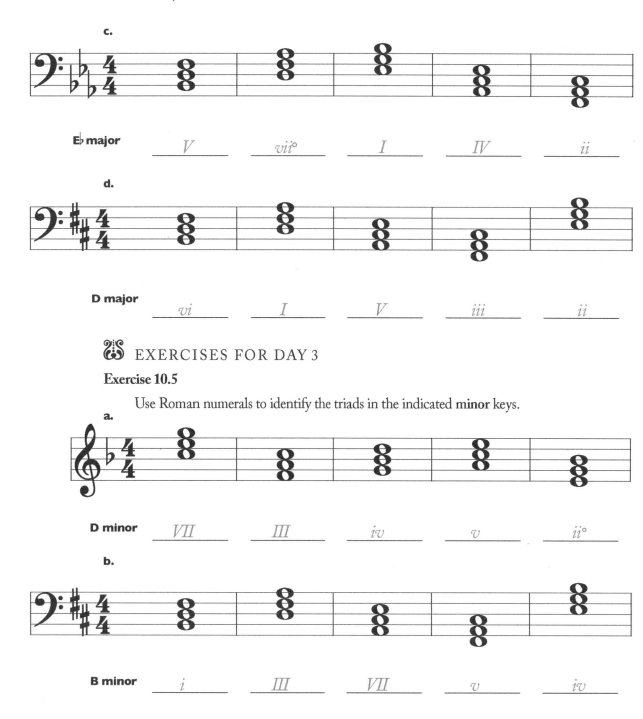

**c.**

E♭ major    V    vii°    I    IV    ii

**d.**

D major    vi    I    V    iii    ii

🎼 EXERCISES FOR DAY 3

**Exercise 10.5**

Use Roman numerals to identify the triads in the indicated **minor** keys.

**a.**

D minor    VII    III    iv    v    ii°

**b.**

B minor    i    III    VII    v    iv

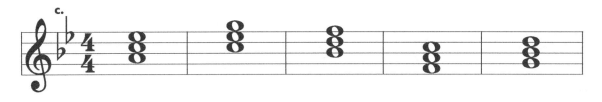

G minor     _ii°_     _iv_     _III_     _VII_     _i_

**Exercise 10.6**

Give Roman numeral analysis to the arpeggiated triads below. The keys are all **major** keys.

_iii_     _ii_     _V_     _vii°_     _I_

_vi_     _IV_     _iii_     _iii_     _ii_

**c.**

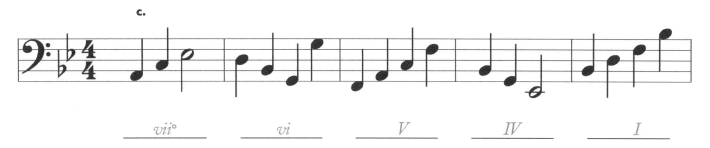

| vii° | vi | V | IV | I |
|------|----|----|----|----|

✿ EXERCISES FOR DAY 4

**Exercise 10.7**

   a)  Label the triads below by letter and quality.

   b)  Label the triads below by triad degree name.

   c)  Label the triads in Roman numeral analysis.

   d)  Transpose the triads to the key of F major. Hint: Follow the steps for transposing from chapter 7. Remember that Roman numeral analysis communicates the scale degree number.

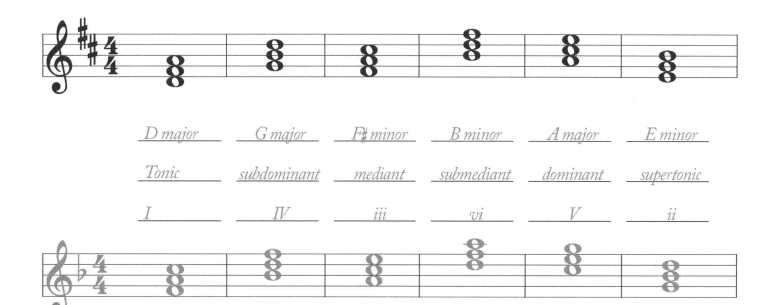

| D major | G major | F♯ minor | B minor | A major | E minor |
|---------|---------|----------|---------|---------|---------|
| Tonic | subdominant | mediant | submediant | dominant | supertonic |
| I | IV | iii | vi | V | ii |

# 11 Triad Inversions

## Chapter 11 Review

```
J  L  X  F  P  U  K  S  J  N
F  I  R  S  T  F  I  I  N  Y
B  K  K  P  R  E  B  G  A  H
G  P  C  T  C  E  U  F  X  V
D  V  B  B  K  A  C  U  R  M
D  N  O  C  E  S  N  O  V  E
W  O  C  G  E  P  O  R  E  B
X  L  U  T  T  T  H  V  C  A
M  G  O  X  T  P  X  E  X  H
F  D  F  A  R  Q  I  M  Y  E
```

## Daily Exercises for Chapter 11

In these exercises for working with inversions, there will be no minor keys.  All of the examples in your exercises will be major key signatures.

### EXERCISES FOR DAY 1

**Exercise 11.1**

Rewrite the root position triads below into first and second inversion triads.

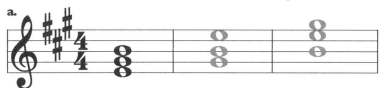

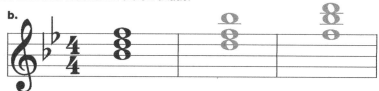

Rewrite the second inversion triads into root position triads.

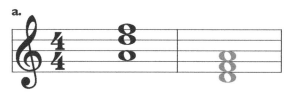

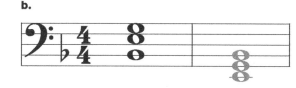

**Exercise 11.2**

Identify the following triads as root, first, or second inversions.

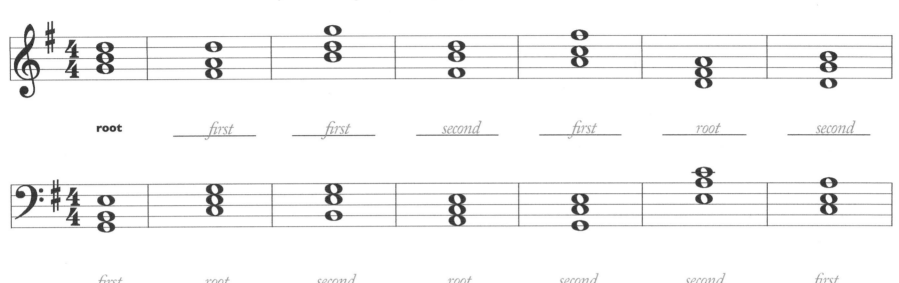

root      *first*      *first*      *second*      *first*      *root*      *second*

*first*      *root*      *second*      *root*      *second*      *second*      *first*

## ❧ EXERCISES FOR DAY 2

**Exercise 11.3**

  a)  Label the triads below by letter and quality.

  b)  Label the triads below by triad degree name.

  c)  Label the triads in Roman numeral analysis including inversion type.

  d)  Transpose the triads into the key of D major. Hint: Follow the steps for transposing from chapter 7. Remember that Roman numeral analysis communicates the scale degree number.

| a) | **D minor** | D minor | D minor | A dim | F major | C minor | B♭ major |
| b) | **mediant** | mediant | mediant | leading tone | dominant | supertonic | tonic |
| c) | **iii$^5_3$** | iii$^6_4$ | iii$^6$ | vii$^{o5}_3$ | V$^6$ | ii$^6$ | I$^5_3$ |

**Exercise 11.4**

Label the following triads with Roman numeral analysis, indicating the type of inversion. Make sure you note the key signatures. Both are major keys.

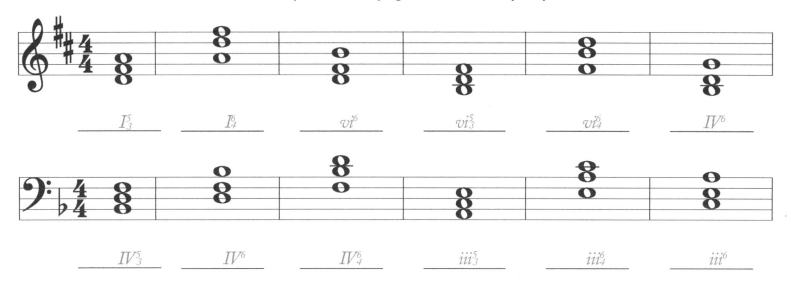

$I^5_3$      $I^6_4$      $vi^6$      $vi^5_3$      $vi^6_4$      $IV^6$

$IV^5_3$      $IV^6$      $IV^6_4$      $iii^5_3$      $iii^6_4$      $iii^6$

❧ EXERCISES FOR DAY 3

**Exercise 11.5**

Rewrite the following augmented and diminished triads into first and second inversions.

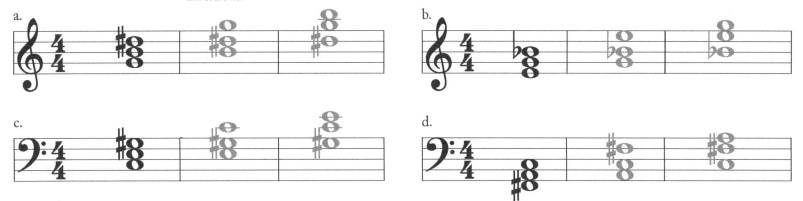

Label the following augmented or diminished triads below as either root, first inversion, or second inversion.

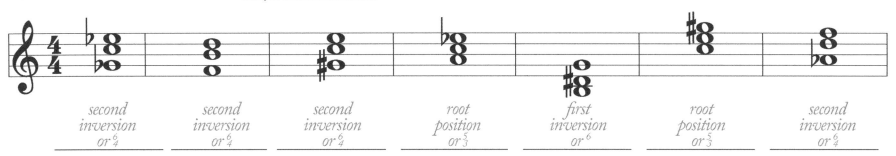

*second inversion or* 6/4       *second inversion or* 6/4       *second inversion or* 6/4       *root position or* 5/3       *first inversion or* 6       *root position or* 5/3       *second inversion or* 6/4

**Exercise 11.6**

Finish writing the triads indicated by the Roman numeral analysis. The given note is the lowest-sounding pitch. Assume each staff is in a major key (not minor). Add sharps or flats as needed to form the indicated triads.

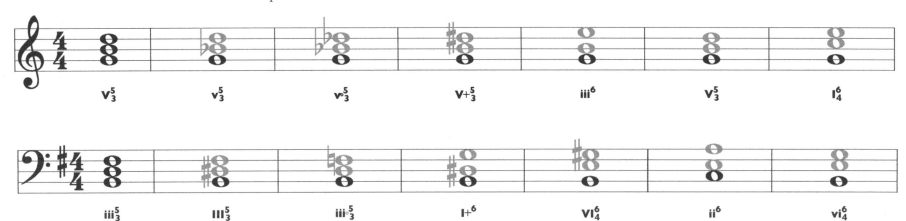

✵ EXERCISES FOR DAY 4

**Exercise 11.7**

Label the following triads with Roman numeral analysis, indicating the type of inversion. Make sure you note the key signature. Assume each staff is in a major key.

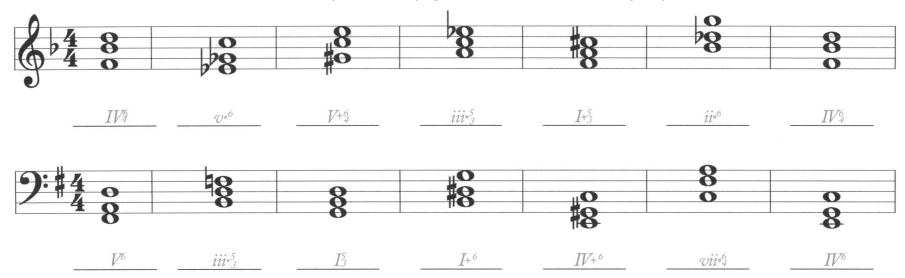

**Exercise 11.8 Advanced Theory (Brain Teasers)**

Build the specified triad above the given bass note. If the note does not contain an accidental, it is meant to be natural. The key signatures are not given or needed. The types of inversions will indicate all you need to give the correct triad and quality. If there are no inversion number(s), it is a root position. Do not be impatient; this exercise will take you some time. Use your keyboard sheet if needed. Write the name of each triad above the notated triad as noted in the examples below.

Aug = augmented        dim = diminished        m = minor        M = major

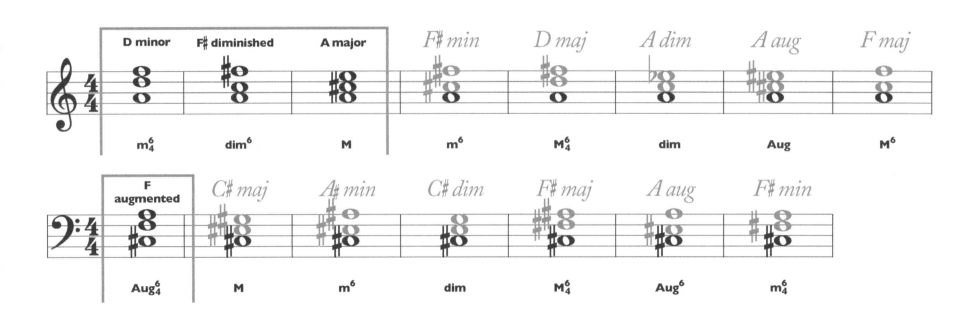

# 12 Score Analysis

Chapters 6–12 Review

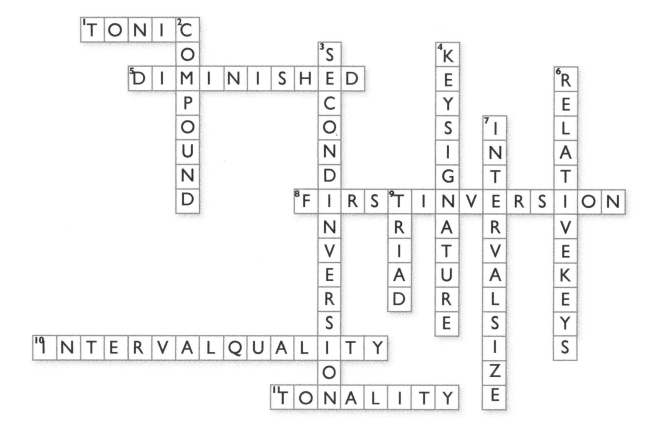

## Daily Exercises for Chapter 12
### ❧ EXERCISES FOR DAY 1

**Exercise 12.1**

Use both the bass and treble clefs to analyze the type of triad in the scores below (but do not yet write out the inversion). Write out the notes.

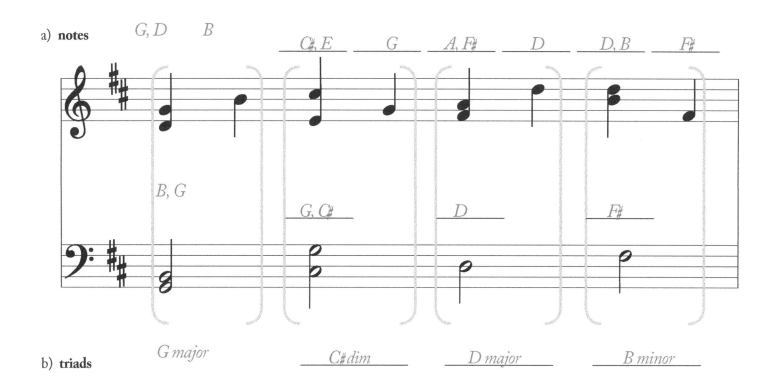

**Exercise 12.2**

Use the notes below to identify the type of triad in each group of notes (e.g., G major). Inversion should not be given.

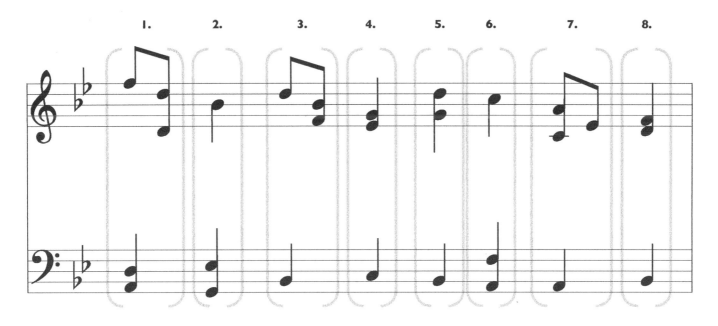

1. *D minor*                                  2. *E♭ major*

3. *B♭ major*                                 4. *C minor*

5. *G minor*                                  6. *F major*

7. *A diminished*                             8. *B♭ major*

❧ EXERCISES FOR DAY 2

**Exercise 12.3**

Label the type of triad in each group of notes below. Each group of notes contains "extra" notes. Circle the "extra" note and list it next to the triad name. The first one has been completed for you.

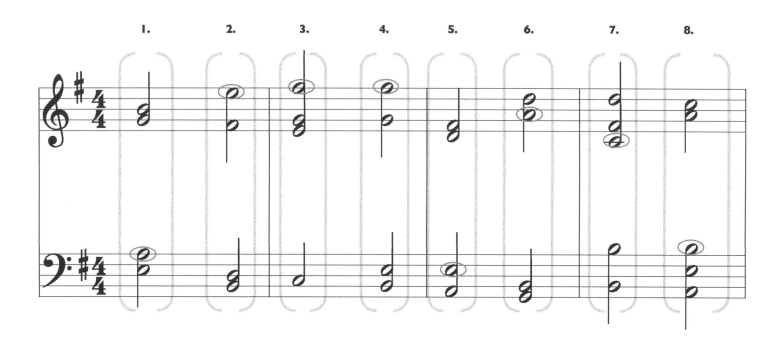

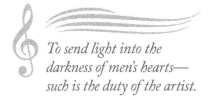

*To send light into the darkness of men's hearts— such is the duty of the artist.*

—Robert Schumann

1. _E minor, A_

2. _B minor, E_

3. _C major, F♯_

4. _E minor, F♯_

5. _D major, E_

6. _G major, A_

7. _B minor, C_

8. _A minor, B_

**Exercise 12.4**

Label the type of triad in each group of notes below. Note that all of these groups of notes have implied notes. Mark the position of the "implied" note(s) with an "x" and list it next to the triad name.

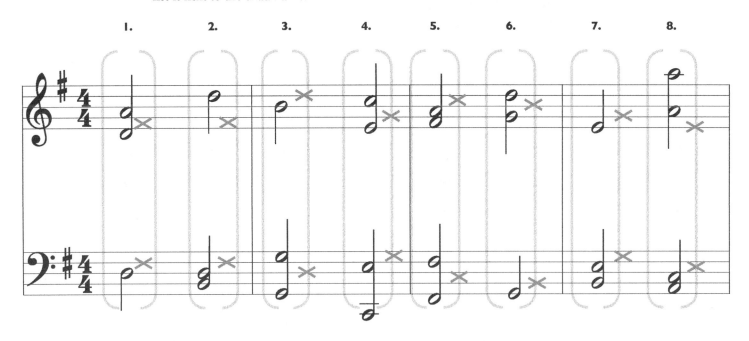

1. *D major, F♯*            2. *B minor, F♯*

3. *G major, D*             4. *C major, G*

5. *F♯ diminished, C*       6. *G major, B*

7. *E minor, G*             8. *A minor, E*

## ❦ EXERCISES FOR DAY 3

**Exercise 12.5**

Use Roman numerals and inversion numbers in your analysis for the groups of notes indicated below in this excerpt from "When I Survey the Wondrous Cross." The lowest note in each group of notes will help you determine the inversion type.

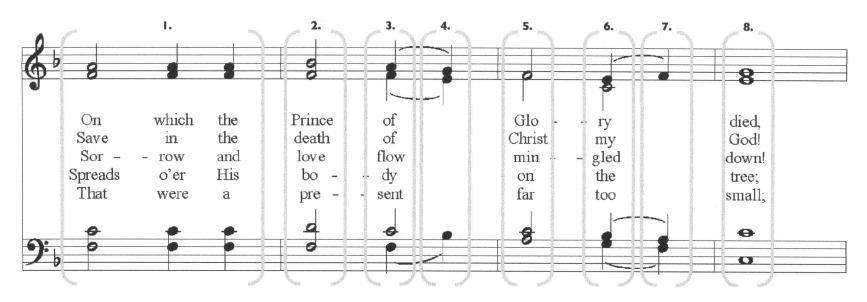

*The C half note in group 3 carries over to beat 4.*

1. _____ $I_3^5$ _____      2. _____ $IV_4^6$ _____      3. _____ $I_3^5$ _____

4. _____ $viio_4^6$ or $V_3^5$ _____      5. _____ $I^6$ _____      6. _____ $V_4^6$ _____

7. _____ $I_3^5$ _____      8. _____ $V_3^5$ _____

**Exercise 12.6**

Use Roman numerals and inversion numbers in your analysis for the groups of notes
indicated below in this excerpt from "There Is a Fountain."

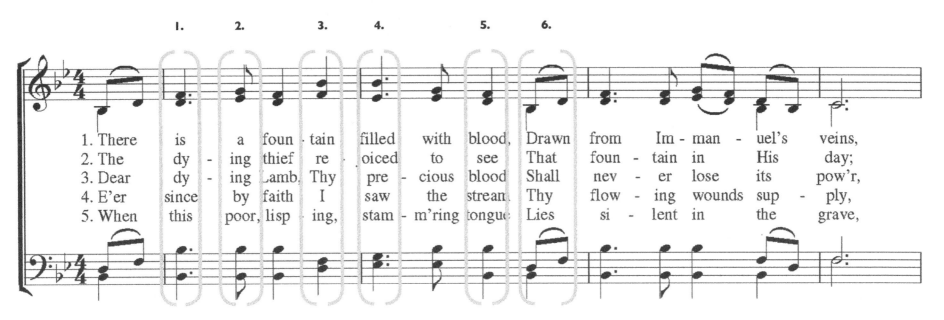

1. $\underline{I^5_3}$  2. $\underline{IV^6_4}$  3. $\underline{I^6}$

4. $\underline{IV^5_3}$  5. $\underline{I^5_3}$  6. $\underline{I^5_3}$

✥ EXERCISES FOR DAY 4

**Exercise 12.7**

Transpose the excerpt from "When I Survey the Wondrous Cross" below into the key of D major. You may want to transfer the Roman numerals from Day 3 Exercise 12.5 to this page before beginning. Hint: Follow the steps for transposing from chapter 7. Remember that Roman numeral analysis communicates the scale degree number.

| | | | | | | | |
|---|---|---|---|---|---|---|---|
| On | which | the | Prince | of | Glo — | - ry | died, |
| Save | in | the | death | of | Christ | my | God! |
| Sor – | - row | and | love | flow | min – | - gled | down! |
| Spreads | o'er | His | bo – | - dy | on | the | tree; |
| That | were | a | pre – | - sent | far | too | small; |

 Score Analyses

# Be Thou My Vision

CONSECRATION

*Words: Attr. Dallan Forgaill, 6th Century. Translated by Mary Byrne, 1905 and Eleanor Hall, 1912.*
*Music: "Slane" Traditional Irish. Setting: Mark Hamilty Dewey, 2007.*
*copyright: public domain. This score is a part of the Open Hymnal Project, 2008 Revision.*

*Key Signature: E♭ major*

*Time Signature: $\frac{3}{4}$ (3 beats per measure with
   the quarter note getting the beat)*

*Relative Key Signature: C minor*

*Intervals labeled above with boxes*

*Score analysis below*

**PH = Project Help,** *Math in Motion* **appendix**

*Jn 16:13, Num 12:6*

*10 10 10 10*

# Jesu, Joy of Man's Desiring

Johann Sebastian Bach
Classical Conversations®, Inc. Edition

Key Signature: *D major*

Time Signature: $\frac{9}{8}$ *(3 beats per measure with the dotted quarter note getting the beat)*

Relative Key Signature: *B minor*

Intervals labeled above with boxes

Score analysis below

*PH = Project Help, *Math in Motion* appendix

# 44. Old Hundredth

## (From All That Dwells Below the Skies)

*This famous tune in the style of a German choral first appeared in the Geneva Psalter about 1555. The four lines of the Doxology were written by Bishop Thomas Ken (1637–1711). The other set of words given here were written by Isaac Watts (1674–1748), one of the greatest of English hymn writers.*

Thos. Ken
Isaac Watts

Louis Bourgeois (?)

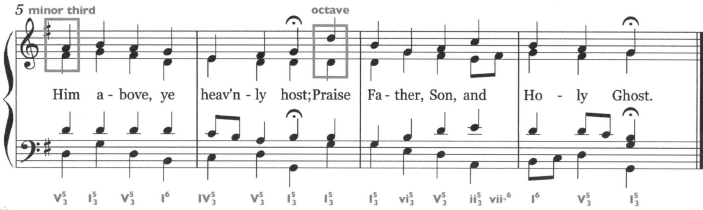

*Key Signature: G major*

*Time Signature: $\frac{4}{4}$ (4 beats per measure with the quarter note getting the beat)*

*Relative Key Signature: E minor*

*Intervals labeled above with boxes*

*Score analysis below*

**\*PH = Project Help,** *Math in Motion* **appendix**

Copyright, 1917, by
C. C. Birchard & Company

**Source:** Dykema, Peter, Will Earhart, Osbourne McConathy, and Hollis Dann. *I Hear America Singing; 55 Songs and Choruses for Community Singing.* Boston,: C. C. Birchard & Company, 1917.

# There Is a Fountain

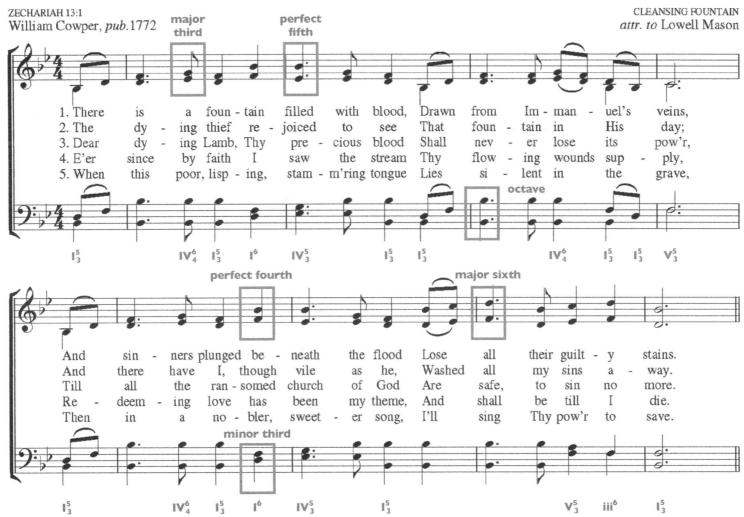

PUBLIC DOMAIN

*Key Signature: Bb major*

*Time Signature: 4/4 (4 beats per measure with the quarter note getting the beat)*

*Relative Key Signature: G minor*

*Intervals labeled above with boxes*

*Score analysis below*

**\*PH = Project Help, *Math in Motion* appendix**

# When I Survey the Wondrous Cross

LENT

*Words: Isaac Watts, 1707.*
*Music: 'Hamburg', Lowell Mason, 1824. Setting: "Northfield Hymnal", 1904.*
*copyright: public domain. This score is a part of the Open Hymnal Project, 2014 Revision.*

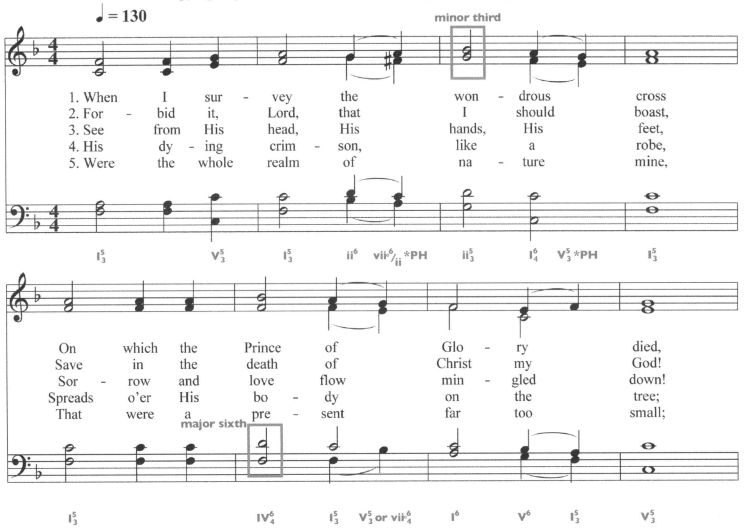

*Key Signature: F major*

*Time Signature: $\frac{4}{4}$ (4 beats per measure with the quarter note getting the beat)*

*Relative Key Signature: D minor*

*Intervals labeled above with boxes*

*Score analysis below*

**\*PH = Project Help, *Math in Motion* appendix**

# When Peace Like a River

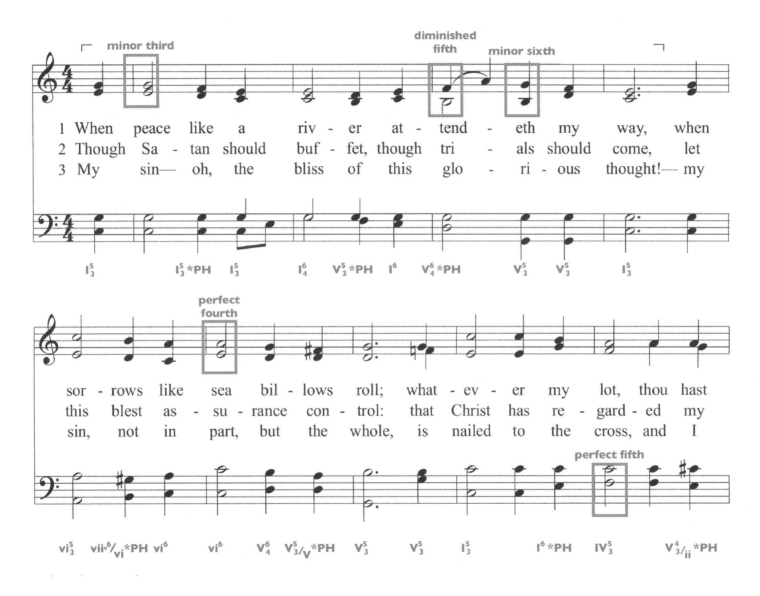

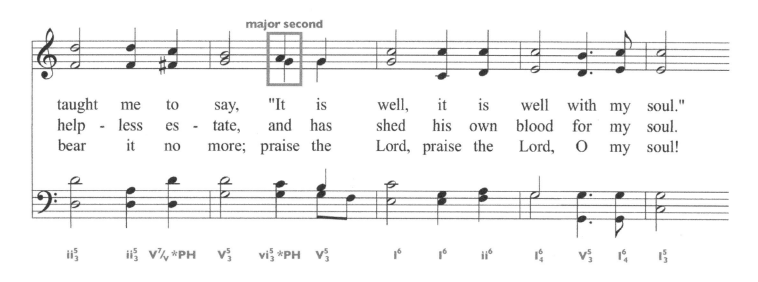

Key Signature: *C major*

Time Signature: $\frac{4}{4}$ *(4 beats per measure with the quarter note getting the beat)*

Relative Key Signature: *A minor*

Intervals labeled above with boxes

Score analysis below

**\*PH = Project Help,** *Math in* **Motion appendix**

Text: Horatio G. Spafford, 1873
Tune: Philip P. Bliss, 1876

11 8 11 9 with refrain
VILLE DU HAVRE
www.hymnary.org/text/when_peace_like_a_river_attendeth_my_way

*Refrain (may be sung after final stanza only)*